THE FORGOTTEN BOTTOM REMEMBERED: STORIES FROM A PHILADELPHIA NEIGHBORHOOD

AUGUST TA   EDITOR

SUSAN B. HYATT, PROJECT DIRECTOR

NEIGHBORHOOD ACTION RESEARCH GROUP

THE FORGOTTEN BOTTOM NEIGHBORHOOD ASSOCIATION

NEW CITY PRESS, 2003

New City Press
ISBN: 0-9712996-4-1

Cover design by Jaeyun Jung
Cover photo credit: Rita Bernstein
Back cover photo credit: RA Friedman
On the back cover (top photo, left to right): Selista Hudson, John Olszewski, Elizabeth Rhodes; (bottom photo, left to right): William Elliott, Edward Gora

To order books from New City Press:
215-204-7347 (phone)
215-204-5015 (fax)
newcity@temple.edu
1114 W. Berks Street
10th Floor Anderson Hall
Philadelphia PA 19122
www.newcitypress.org

The Community Publishing class and neighborhood residents in front of a mural at 34th and Wharton, 2002

The students who participated in this project were: Julie Duffield, Nicole Fox, Valarie Greene, Christie Hochrine, Jennifer Iacovelli, Jessica Maley, Markia McClenton, Ryan Murphy, Tiffany Patterson, Jennifer Reilly, Natia Robinson, Susanna Stewart, Melton Thomas, and Stefanie Woolridge.

3

PREFACE

I am very pleased to be writing this preface to the second edition of *The Forgotten Bottom Rememberered*. In the course of working on the first edition, both community residents and Temple faculty recognized that a collaborative project of this nature requires a great deal of trust and cooperation. None of us had ever participated in an adventure such as this, and we were at first skeptical as to its outcome, but flattered that we were asked to become part of an oral history project that would document our lives.

When we first met the students who conducted the life histories, we gave them a walking tour of the neighborhood so that they could bear witness with us to the forces that had molded us. We told them of the circumstances and the events that had shaped the culture of the community and that determined the kinds of people who have lived and continue to live here.

We knew we were in a unique position—a city neighborhood that was not predominantly of one race, culture, or religion. This is neighborhood that, despite its location within the larger neighborhood known as Grays Ferry, has never, in all its many years of existence, undergone the racial strife that has characterized the history and recent past of the other blocks of Grays Ferry east of 34th Street.

We were proud that many of the families that had moved here from the beginning of the early 'teens and twenties of the past century were still living in the very same houses or in nearby houses that their parents or other relatives had occupied. We had a story to tell, a story that not only was one of racial harmony, but one that would also be a model for the rest of the City to emulate.

Since the publication of the first edition in autumn 2002, Mr. Fred Kent, owner of Bessie's Chicken Shack, has passed away. Mr. Edward Gora, who served long and faithfully as Vice President of the Forgotten Bottom Neighborhood Association, is gravely ill and unable to participate in our monthly meetings. Mr. and Mrs.

William Elliott are now in a nursing home as a result of a horrific automobile accident that happened last December 30, 2002. And Mrs. MacClain, always famous for her cookies, has since left the neighborhood and has relocated to a retirement community.

These changes in the lives of the people whose stories are chronicled in this book make all of us realize how precious the ties are that have bound us together as friends and neighbors for all these many years. While individuals' circumstances change, sometimes sadly so, our community remains the kind of place it has always been: accepting, tolerant and always willing to give people who mean well a second chance.

I am most grateful to my community and the officers of the Forgotten Bottom Neighborhood Association for permitting me to serve as their president for the last six years. I would like to thank the following people for all of their support and encouragement: Mr. and Mrs. Romeo Rivello whom I have known practically all of my life; Mr. John Olszewski who is my "running buddy" and who has known me since I was a very young girl; and Mr. William Elliott, who has been my surrogate father, counselor, and mentor for more years than I can count.

I would also like to thank Dr. Stephen Parks who called numerous times and met with me and put up with my many missed deadlines asking, "What can New City Press do to make this book right?" I also thank Susan Hyatt and August Tarrier for the work they put into this project.

The Forgotten Neighborhood Association would not nor could not exist without the able help of its officers: Mr. Edward Gora, Vice President; Mr. Romeo Rivello, Sergeant at Arms; Mr. William Elliott, Chaplain; Mrs. Selista Hudson, Treasurer; and Ms. Lena Clarkson, Secretary.

Marilyn A. Brown
President, Forgotten Bottom Neighborhood Association
June 2003

A street in the Forgotten Bottom

T he Forgotten Bottom is a community located in South Philadelphia: it is west of 34th Street and is comprised of about 15 residential blocks hemmed in by 34th St. and I-76 to the east, the Schuylkill River to the west, Grays Ferry Avenue to the north, and vacant industrial and railroad land to the south. Much of the housing stock is old and many of its most active community residents are now senior citizens. The Forgotten Bottom neighborhood is unique, however, not only for the longevity of residence of most of its inhabitants, many of whom grew up there, but also for the strength of the bonds that have united people across racial and ethnic boundaries for many years. Although officially the community is considered

Harmony Street in the Forgotten Bottom

part of the neighborhood known as Grays Ferry, residents of the Forgotten Bottom pride themselves on having avoided the racial conflict and turmoil that has characterized much of the community east of 34th Street.

It was in the spring of 2001 that Susan B. Hyatt, a professor of Anthropology at Temple University, first became acquainted with residents of the Forgotten Bottom through a larger ethnographic fieldwork project. On one occasion, when she was present at a monthly meeting of the Forgotten Bottom Neighborhood Association, neighborhood residents expressed a desire to have the history of their community recorded and published. Intrigued by this idea, Hyatt discussed the possibilities with August Tarrier, a professor of English at Temple and Editor of New City Press, a community press housed at Temple. Tarrier jumped at the chance to work on the project.

During Spring Semester 2002, Tarrier and Hyatt organized an oral history project focused on capturing stories from the neighborhood. Working together, we trained students enrolled in Tarrier's Community Publishing course to conduct local research and interview residents. One bright and sunny day in February, we brought the students down to the Forgotten Bottom so that they could see the neighborhood and meet the residents for the first time. It was love at first sight for all parties involved. Several neighborhood residents took time out of their busy schedules to give the students a walking tour of the community. Helen MacClain treated us to her homemade cookies, for which she is rightfully famous in local circles! (Some of her favorite recipes are included in this book.) Lena Clarkson, Selista and James Hudson, Lillian Ray, and John Olszewski were our knowledgeable guides. After our first visit to the community, the students were even more enthusiastic about the project. "Thank you so much for making us feel so at home," one of them wrote on a card we later sent to the Forgotten Bottom Neighborhood Association. "This is just what a real neighborhood should be like," remarked another.

Everyone involved in this project—professors, students, residents and other volunteers—worked together to produce a book which showcases the lives of community residents through oral life histories (recorded and transcribed by our students), historical documents, recipes, letters and photographs.

The Forgotten Bottom Remembered is a tribute to a neighborhood which by its very nature provides inspiration for other urban communities. Through our encounter with the Forgotten Bottom, we have experienced firsthand the residents' love for their community and for their neighbors. As Mr. Edward Gora said, "We're one big family." Lillian Ray, another longtime resident, told us, "Down here we all ate together, slept together and kept our doors open." When we asked how the community managed to foster such strong bonds, Lena Clarkson summed it up this way: "One family is not going to watch another family suffer." Perhaps Raymond Baines explained it best when, standing in front of his house on Harmony Street, he said "There's harmony on this corner."

As always, with any undertaking of this magnitude, we have many people to

August Tarrier (l) and Susan Hyatt (r) talking with neighborhood residents John Olszewski, Ed Gora and William Elliott.

thank. In her capacity as President of the Forgotten Bottom Neighborhood Association, Marilyn Brown was invaluable in her support for the project and in facilitating many of the logistics. Joe Taggart and the other folks at St. John's Club provided a base for our operations and never failed to be helpful and accommodating. The contemporary photographs in the book were taken by Rita Bernstein and RA Friedman. Fred Barrett provided technical support for the scanning of the historical photos and documents, and Peter Hanley helped us create the website we used for storing our work-in-progress. The book was designed by Jaeyun Jung.

Margaret Jerrido and Evan Towle of the Urban Archives at Temple's Paley Library were extremely helpful in locating maps and documents for us and in guiding students through the intricacies of archival research. Likewise, social science librarian Greg McKinney also helped us to find background material on the history of Philadelphia's neighborhoods. Financial support for this project was provided by a grant from the Knight Foundation to New City Writing at Temple University. We also thank Dean Morris Vogel of the College of Liberal Arts at Temple for his support for this—and many other—undertakings.

Lastly, we would like to thank the residents of the Forgotten Bottom, many of whose life histories are included in this book. We have included interviews with thirteen residents here; with more time and resources, we could have presented many more. We hope the stories we have published here will do justice to the collective hearts and spirits of all the people of the Forgotten Bottom, a unique Philadelphia neighborhood which will always be remembered by those of us who were fortunate enough to become a part of its history for even a short time, and who were honored to be asked to tell its stories.

August Tarrier and Susan Brin Hyatt

TAKING CARE OF BUSINESS

BY MELTON THOMAS

P hiladelphia, Pennsylvania is known worldwide as the "City of Brotherly Love," but anyone who has ever visited knows that Philadelphia is about family, history and its preservation. No place in the city better captures this theme than the Forgotten Bottom. Located on the outskirts of the Grays Ferry area of Southwest Philadelphia, this small neighborhood has big character and family structure amongst the shadows of the factories that used to saturate the area with business and activity. Now, the doors have closed and the residents of the Forgotten Bottom have found new reasons to take pride in the stock of their neighborhood. The peace and calm of quiet, family-based living prevails. Bessie's Chicken Shack has always shone bright as a beacon of hope that exemplifies family-centric life in its history, food and even its proprietor.

Fletcher Kent is the proprietor of Bessie's Chicken Shack, a family owned soul food restaurant with atmosphere to please the soul and food to please the appetite. Located at 3530 Wharton Street, Bessie's sits as a warm welcome into the Forgotten Bottom area. Keeping it in the family, Kent has taken over the business from the hands of his parents Fred and Bessie Kent who this year will celebrate the 35th anniversary of its opening.

"Wow, thirty-five years. That's a long time!" was the only reaction I could muster after contemplating one small family-owned business that has become an institution in a neighborhood where home-cooked meals are a given. Bessie's opened on September 1st, 1967. The business stemmed from Fred Kent's work at Consolidated Dressed Beef, which was on the other side of Grays Ferry Avenue. Fletcher Kent remembers, "They [Fred and Bessie] used to sell dinners and stuff to the guys at work because at night they wanted something to eat. Then they located this property here [3530 Wharton St.] and bought it and started from there." And from there Bessie's has been making history in the Forgotten Bottom ever since with very few changes.

Upon opening, Bessie ran the kitchen. She did everything from plan the menu, cook the food and offer a welcoming smile to all who entered the doors. Fred Kent would handle the finances of the business and facilitate all the ordering. Together the two were a perfect team running a well-oiled machine that could only be maintained with good business sense, great tasting food and love. Sadly, Bessie Kent passed away in 2000, but her spirit will forever live on in her loved ones, Fred and Fletcher, the Forgotten Bottom, and everyone who has or ever will eat at Bessie's and experience the love that continues to come from her kitchen. Now the cooking is done by another generation of Kents.

Fletcher Kent never entered the kitchen of Bessie's Chicken Shack until he was 16 years old; however, he had firsthand experience in Bessie's kitchen at his childhood residence at 6th and Cantrell. When he wasn't out enjoying his youth, he was in the kitchen learning the ways of his mother. Kent parlayed those lessons into an ability to give people what they want —"a good solid meal."

He and his mom have changed little about the way the food is prepared in the last 35 years, even looking out for the health and welfare of others. "We do use different spices because we have a lot of people that don't eat meat, who don't eat pork, so that was eliminated a long time ago. We simply

Editor August Tarrier interviews Mr. Fred Kent at his restaurant, Bessie's Chicken Shack.

just jazz it up with spices. We've toned down the salt, because everybody in my family has had or has high blood pressure, even the some of the guys working here."

Fletcher Kent continues to serve the people of the Forgotten Bottom under the guidance and watchful eye of his father Fred Kent and will continue to do so indefinitely. And they must be doing something right. Bessie's has been crowded since the doors first opened. Not only did they draw an African American crowd, the customers were representative of the diversity of the neighborhood, including German, Irish, and Polish. The Kents attribute the mixed crowd to the "highway" [the Schuylkill], which served as a boundary from the racial tensions east of 34th Street. The Kent family has served the community for 35 years this September. They have survived the de-industrialization of the neighborhood, the turbulent times of the '70s, the Reagan-Era Recession, and the economic tech boom of the '90s, to emerge into the 21st century as a neighborhood fixture in their own little "Mayberry." According to Kent, the cops refer to the Forgotten Bottom as "Mayberry" because of the lack of crime in the area. It seems to have sparked a glow in Fletcher Kent's face for him to say, "You don't have too much of any crime in this area, hardly any." He continues, "well, you know, they [the police] come around. I see them, but they hardly ever get a call from down here. Every once and awhile." He, like members of the community, takes pride in the existence of the Forgotten Bottom as a peaceful entity that has avoided the perils and hang-ups of the outside world.

Even Bessie's, with 35 years in the same location, with the same management, and same menu, can't escape the events of the world that change us all. September 11, 2001, that unforgettable date, has marked not only our calendars but also our hearts. And for business owners like the Kents, it marked their checkbooks. Kent states," Well, the economy was going down before that, and it seems that September 11th just stepped it up. People were afraid to come out and spend money. If people aren't spending money, people are being laid off." He continues with an allegory based somewhat in the measures of his own business. "We used to go through maybe 120 loaves of bread a week, now we're lucky if we go through 85—80. That goes back to the bakery—35-40 loaves that they're not making, so they don't need that other baker. That baker who wanted to remodel his house can't do it because he's out of a job. So in turn, the home-repairman can't earn his living because the guy can't pay him. So it's like a spiral effect." This shows the strict interrelationship of various types of business and the dependence on every customer for their continued longevity.

This longevity is threatened by dangerous external factors and a couple of ghosts from the neighborhood's past. The abandonment of the surrounding companies that once thrived in the area serves as a new point of interest after environmental dangers were discovered from the ways of industry. High rates of asbestos where found in the factory shells that were once filled with many people from the area daily; Fletcher Kent believes this to have caused many cancerous deaths, usually lung cancer, of ex-factory employees. Lackadaisical restrictions on chemical waste disposal are an important factor that has even alerted the EPA to the neighborhood time has forgotten. The government agency was in the area testing groundwater before the ground was broken for the newly built Federal Express plant. FedEx is the most recent industry to share the neighborhood with Bessie's but it probably isn't the last. There is no doubt that Bessie's and the Forgotten Bottom community as a whole will continue to uphold their family-oriented ways of life. Bessie's has not been the sole family owned eatery in the Forgotten Bottom. The Shack once shared their customers with various grocery stores, delis, and steak and hoagie shops, all family maintained (one of the first Black-owned businesses in the neighborhood was Brown's Cleaners, started in 1952 and owned by the parents of Marilyn Brown.) The latest addition is Melee's Luncheonette, owned and operated by Mrs. Lillian Ray. §

A year after this interview was completed, Mr. Fred Kent passed away. At the time of this printing, summer 2003, Bessie's Chicken Shack is closed after 35 years in business.

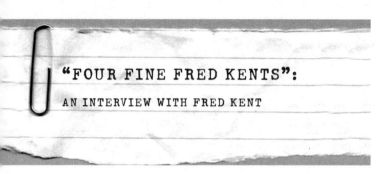

"FOUR FINE FRED KENTS":

AN INTERVIEW WITH FRED KENT

"Nobody else mean nothing to me like she did—she was the star in my life"—Fred Kent

Mr. Fred Kent is the original owner, with his late wife Bessie, of Bessie's Chicken Shack, one of the first Black businesses in the neighborhood. Of his wife, Bessie Fletcher, Mr. Kent says, "she was the sweetest girl in the world." Mr. Kent is now 82 and he told us that when he passes on, he and his wife will be "two angels in heaven together." Clearly still fiercely devoted to his departed wife, Mr. Kent said, "Nobody else mean nothing to me like she did—she was the star in my life." The Kents were married in 1944, right after Fred Kent returned from World War II—he was 24 years old. Bessie died in 2000 and at that time the Kents had been married for 56 years.

Mr. Kent told us the story of their early courtship. Bessie was living in Montgomery, Alabama at the time and Fred lived in Chattanooga, Tennessee, where he "had a little business selling sundries." Mr. Kent said of Bessie: "Her sister knew me—she was a good friend of my cousin. And my cousin said, 'There's a beautiful woman coming up here and you better hurry over here 'cause the guys are gonna grab her.'" And Mr. Kent did hurry over to his cousin's house, where Bessie was staying, but, as he said, "she wouldn't talk to me that day. I sent for her about three times through my cousin, but she wouldn't talk to me. Finally, at the last moment, I said, 'you just tell her that

Louise [his cousin] wants to see her,' so then she did come down. That way I seen her. I said, 'Your sister knows me. I'll show you some things, take you out to the park.' And then I had to get Lilly's [Bessie's aunt] permission and she said, 'Fred, I respect you,' and so then Bessie and me, we went riding the

> **"So after Bessie went back home I wrote a letter to her father and he wrote me back and said, 'My daughter told me that she kinda fell in love with you and she wants to come back to Chattanooga. If you want to marry her, you write me back and I'll think about what kind of young man you are.'"**

buses all over the city. I told her about me having this little stand selling confectioneries and I asked her, 'Would you like to really know me?' and told her, 'Your aunt ain't gonna bother you' and 'I'll talk to your Dad.' So after Bessie went back home I wrote a letter to her father and he wrote me back and said, 'My daughter told me that she kinda fell in love with you and she wants to come back to Chattanooga. If you want to marry her, you write me back and I'll think about what kind of young man you are.' And, boy, I sent my letter back, too! I said, 'Mr. Fletcher, if you let Bessie come back here, you'll never have a problem with her.' I told him, 'I kinda fell in love with her these past three weeks.' And he got the letter and called to talk to my

Memorial to Bessie Fletcher-Kent, lovingly maintained by her husband, Mr. Fred Kent, in their restaurant, Bessie's Chicken Shack.

mother. He said, 'You got a boy who's kinda strong and he talks to me like he knows what he's doing, so I'm gonna send my daughter up there. And I'm expecting you to treat my daughter right.' And we went right on from there. In six months to a year we were married."

Mr. Kent gave a satisfied smile and said, "That's my story. I done lived my life as a family man. I raised two great sons—Fred, Jr. and Fletcher. I don't fret about nothin'. I talk to the Master every night. I can't go to sleep without talking to God and thanking him for blessing me. There's four fine Fred Kents in this world: my father was Fred Kent, I'm Fred Kent, my first born is Fred Kent and his second son is Fred Kent." §

"There's four fine Fred Kents in this world: my father was Fred Kent, I'm Fred Kent, my first born is Fred Kent and his second son is Fred Kent."

"A GOOD SOLID MEAL":

AN INTERVIEW WITH FLETCHER KENT,

PROPRIETOR OF BESSIE'S CHICKEN SHACK

BY MELTON THOMAS

MELTON THOMAS: First, can you tell me your name and a brief bio of yourself.

FLETCHER KENT: Fletcher Kent, proprietor of Bessie's Chicken Shack. Bessie Kent and Fred Kent have long been—Bessie Kent has since deceased September of 2000 and I have taken over the business, although Fred Kent is still here and working.

MT: When was the business started?

FK: September 1, 1967.

MT: Was it hard for your parents coming into this neighborhood starting anew or were they already located in the neighborhood?

FK: No. No, my father used to work at the Consolidated Dressed Beef, which was on Grays Ferry Ave. many years ago. They used to sell dinners and stuff to the guys at work because at night they wanted something to eat. Then they located this property here and bought it and started from there.

MT: Now starting out, was it easy

going, say, getting a loan and things like that?

FK: No. It's never easy starting out a business, especially in the restaurant business, getting loans. But collateral was—they had a house on 6th and Cantrell St.

MT: When they started, it was just a spin-off of your father bringing your mother's dinners to work?

FK: Right. And basically the menu on the steam table hasn't changed in 35 years.

MT: Wow, 35 years—that's a long time! Have the prices changed?

FK: Definitely! We're still priced below most other places, but that's the neighborhood.

MT: How was it growing up around here? I'm sure you grew up probably in the kitchen of this place?

FK: Well, yes, basically.
The neighborhood is fairly quiet. It's really no problem, just about everybody gets along. But I didn't spend my—Well, I came up here when I was in high school. So when

I wasn't in here I was out other places. By that time, I wasn't spending too much time in the neighborhood. I had friends on the block, we would run someplace and what have you.

MT: Now, when you came up here, was that from "Down South" or the 6th and Cantrell house?

FK: 6th and Cantrell.

MT: What about this area? When you came as a teenager what did you think walking the streets?

FK: Um, a little quiet. You had to travel to do anything. There was not much to do around here.

MT: So as a teenager what did you do, like, when you did come back to the area?

FK: I was basically in the house. Or I would go to a neighbor's house.

MT: Did you live above the restaurant?

FK: Yes, I did, and my father still does.

MT: Where do you reside now?

FK: In Center City, until—until Pop [Fred Kent] needs my help.

MT: What did you do after high school? Where'd you go after leaving this area?

FK: Well, there was some schooling, but I had to stop that to come back into the business. And I was

Melton Thomas in front of Bessie's Chicken Shack at Wharton and Grove, 2002

here just about every day.

MT: Did you do work as the proprietor or just a worker?

FK: Yes, manager, whatever.

MT: Did you get paid as a manager?

FK: Yes, it was a formal job with formal managerial pay.

MT: How was it running the family business? Was there a mixed crowd that came in to enjoy the food?

FK: Always! Always a mixed crowd. Which is a blessing, actually, because you figure back during then there was a lot more industry around you. You had Barrett's Roofing Consolidated, Oscar Meyer, Dupont was larger, the railroad employed a lot more people, we had two or three factories back behind it, and a lot of them would come here to eat. We had the bar on the corner, they would stop there—

MT: Tony D's?

FK: Well, that's what it is now. So that made for a mixed crowd and this neighborhood was fairly mixed.

MT: Yes, I've noticed that. With the area being mixed, how was your business affected by the riots of the 1990's that occurred on the other side of Grays Ferry?

FK: Actually, no. All that stopped at 34th St. across the highway. A lot of people were talking about it but still it wasn't a big issue over here, among the people living around here because they realized this was a neighborhood.

MT: Now, being that the highway is located right there, it sort of dissects you from the rest of the Grays Ferry area. Is that a blessing or a hindrance?

FK: That's a blessing. You don't have too much of any crime in this area, hardly any. Even the police call it "Mayberry"—nothing goes on in here.

MT: Is there a police presence at all?

FK: Yes, well, you know, they come around. I see them, but they hardly ever get a call from down here. Every once and awhile.

MT: Is there a significant number of youth in the neighborhood?

FK: Yes, there are a lot of children.

MT: What's your favorite thing on the menu?

FK: [laughs] You mean, when I could eat it [laughs]? Fried chicken, baked macaroni and candied yams the way Mom made them then and the way I make them now.

MT: Did you make any improvements to any of your mom's recipes?

FK: No, I don't think so. Because people are going back to the basics and want a good solid meal.

MT: We all know that soul food

" . . . We used to go through maybe 120 loaves of bread a week, now we're lucky if we go through 85—80. That goes back to the bakery, 35-40 loaves that they're not making so they don't need that other baker. That baker who wanted to remodel his house can't do it because he's out of a job. So in turn, the home repairman can't do it because the guy can't pay him."

isn't known for being the most health conscious, so what do you—what types of meats do you use for your greens?

FK: We don't. We do use different spices because we have a lot of people that don't eat meat, who don't eat pork, so that was eliminated a long time ago. We simply just jazz it up with spices. We've toned down the salt because everybody in my family has had or has high blood pressure, even some of the guys working here. So the salt was terribly toned down.

MT: But it hasn't lost any of its flavor, has it?

FK: No, we eat here everyday [laughs], twice a day, sometimes three, in my case.

MT: Do you ever want to eat something else?

FK: All the time, I've been seeing this for 35 years, but I don't feel like going out to get it—just something.

MT: Is there usually a steady crowd?

FK: [pauses] It varies. Everybody's business dropped off after 9/11. But it dropped off again after FedEx blocked off the street. It became harder for people to get into this neighborhood: where they used to come right down this street, [now] they have to go another block and they don't realize it [the neighborhood], or they have to come another way and don't realize it [the neighborhood]. Say, if there is an accident that blocks off the street it cuts off the whole neighborhood.

MT: What are some of your feelings about September 11th and the reflection on the declining business?

FK: Well, the economy was going down before that and it seems that September 11th just stepped it up. People were afraid to come out and spend money. If people aren't spending money, people are being laid off. I'll give you, for instance, just one particular item: we used to go through maybe 120 loaves of bread a week, now we're lucky if we go through 85—80. That goes back to the bakery, 35-40 loaves that they're not making so they don't need that other baker. That baker who wanted to remodel his house can't do it because he's out of a job. So in turn, the home repairman can't do it because the guy can't pay him. So it's like a spiral effect. That sharp cut.

MT: How do you feel about Fed-Ex? I heard that they promised 150 jobs—

FK: I haven't seen anybody from this neighborhood.

MT: I heard they promised jobs but then they realized that there are a lot of older people, and hoped to employ their grandchildren and younger people and then they ended up reneging on their job offers. Do you have any feelings about the Fed-Ex Co. as for cutting off the neighborhood a little and for neglecting their promises?

FK: What they've been saying is bullshit because there is a lot of youth on both sides of the expressway. I don't believe they did enough to recruit them. I haven't seen or heard of anyone in this area, in this pocket or the other side, that have been hired by FedEx right here. I know people that have been looking to find work or trying to get their sons a job.

MT: With the construction of the plant or its opening, has that helped business? Like the construction workers or the current workers see you over here and trickle in?

FK: A few, but with them I'd get one or two people, so it hasn't helped at all. It hasn't really helped anybody.

MT: Were the hours always the same?

FK: No. We used to be open a lot later, but I'm only one person. We cut the hours down so we could have a life after work. And we cut out a day. We used to run six days a week, now we're at five. We're off

Sunday and Monday. Monday I can run and get stock and do the little repairs that always need to be done.

MT: What's one of your favorite things to make on the menu?

FK: The baked macaroni and cheese because it takes a little doing the way it was taught to me and the way I do it. A lot of people don't realize.

MT: What about any family-owned businesses in the neighborhood? Were there any? Are there still any?

FK: Not like there was before.

MT: What's before?

FK: You used to have Anne's around the corner—a mother and daughter used to run that. It was like a deli, a little grocery store. You had a steak and hoagie shop across the street from us, run by a brother and sister. Another grocery store that may have since long gone and another steak and hoagie place. All those people that I've named are gone; some have passed away and I don't know what happened to them all.

MT: Is there still a bakery or some kind of business open on the next block?

FK: No, not a bakery. You have some people who came in and do contracting work. You have a garage. And some people who were doing illegal dumping on proper-ties, inside buildings. Across the street where FedEx is you had illegal dumping. They were paid by the city to clean it out, but they had failed and was dumping there too. Then FedEx came along and I don't know how it worked out, but there is a vacant lot in back and they're dumping there.

MT: What are they dumping?

FK: They say refuse from torn down houses that they get from contracts from the city; however, the EPA was out across the street from here testing the ground soil. I don't know what the previous illegal dumpers are doing. With the illegal dumping you never know what they're dumping, so there's no telling. With heavy industrialization like with Barrett's they used a lot of asbestos. And a lot of the guys that I used to know that work there have since died from cancer, whether it be lung cancer or what have you. I think that's due to the asbestos that they worked in. I don't know about the cluster rate in this one pocket but who knows what pollutants you have from the oil refinery. Further down the river, there was Barrett's Roofing and Dupont, among others. §

Marilyn Brown, 2002

Born May 31, 1938, Marilyn Brown has lived in the Forgotten Bottom neighborhood almost all her life. She attended the Philadelphia public schools and graduated from John Bartram High School in 1956. She earned a Bachelors Degree in Business Education and a Masters in Education in 1972, both at Temple University. Currently, Marilyn Brown is a professor at Community College in Philadelphia, Pennsylvania where she has taught business studies for 33 years. Ms. Brown has a great love of dogs and owns two Rottweilers. She is also currently president of the Forgotten Bottom Neighborhood Association.

"DOUBLE DUTCH QUEEN":

AN INTERVIEW WITH MARILYN BROWN

BY NATIA ROBINSON

"I am proud of my family members. I have a family full of dentists, lawyers, doctors, preachers and tons of teachers."

NR: What year were you born?

MB: I was born in 1938.

NR: How old are you?

MB: I am 63; I'll be 64 on May 31, next month.

NR: Were you born in the neighborhood, the Forgotten Bottom?

MB: No, I was born at 22nd and Christian Streets. That is where my family lived at that time. However, it is part of South Philadelphia.

NR: Where do you live now?

MB: I live on Wharton Street.

NR: When did you move there?

MB: We moved there, I believe, in 1952 or 1951; yeah, I'd say 1952. Before that, we lived at 3441 Reed Street, which is part of the Forgotten Bottom neighborhood. I lived at 22nd and Christian Streets

until I was—what?—two years old. If you want to say that I was born and raised in the Forgotten Bottom neighborhood, you can. I've lived there for 62 years. God, that is a long time.

NR: How many brothers and sisters do you have?

MB: I have two brothers and one sister. My older brother Carl and my sister Cissy are deceased. My younger brother Marvin and I are the only children left.

NR: How did your brother and sister die?

MB: They both died from congestive heart failure; it's a disease that runs in the family. My father died from congestive heart failure, too. My mother was just—she just died of old age.

NR: How old was your mother when she died?

MB: She was in her 84th year when she died.

NR: Do you know where the Forgotten Bottom name originated?

MB: You know, ever since I've lived there, it was called the Bottom. When the Association was formed, about five years ago, someone—and it wasn't me—said: "We're always being forgotten. No one cares that we're down here." Someone else said, "Well, why don't we call our-selves the Forgotten Bottom?" We all agreed. That's the truth and it *is* a very descriptive name. No one ever knew we were down there. The City was almost unaware that our neighborhood existed. You know, it was a miracle we got any City serv-ices. So you know, we were *forgotten*.

NR: What was it like in your neighborhood when you were younger?

MB: When I was younger, it was a great neighborhood. I really enjoyed it. Naturally, all the Blacks lived together and we still do. The whites always lived together. But we all got along fine. There weren't

any racial fights that I was aware of. When I lived on Reed Street, it was an all Black block except for the Basses. When the family moved to Wharton Street in 1952, we were the first Black family on that block. My neighbors were all Italian except for the Bobolopskis, who were Jewish.

NR: Was that the only Jewish family?

MB: Yes, on Wharton Street. When I lived on Reed Street, the Basses, who owned a variety store, were the only Jewish family in that neighbor-hood. Throughout most of my childhood, and as a young adult, the neighborhood was fairly well integrated. We had Germans, Jews, Blacks, Italians, and Polish families. I don't remember if there were any Irish families, but I'm sure there

Marilyn Brown with her new puppy, Sieglinde Agrippina Von Braun, in 1985

were. If I'm not mistaken, most of the Irish families lived below 34th Street.

NR: How do you feel about your neighborhood today?

MB: I still enjoy living there. It has changed a lot; it is noisier and dirtier. The people are still friendly, but I sense they are a lot younger than I am. I am now the "new older people." I don't know them as well. When I was growing up, you knew all of the older people in the neighborhood. It's not like that now. I just know enough to say "Hi."

However, the young people are still respectful of us older folks. We can still—if any of the children cause trouble—we can go to their parents and tell them that so-and-so did this, and their parents will say something to them. The younger parents with younger children, I really don't know them at all. But again, it's still a quiet neighbor hood and a relatively safe neighborhood.

NR: How do you feel about Federal Express?

MB: I think Fed Ex is great. I know

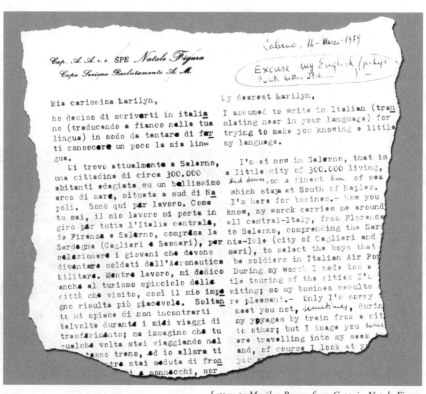

Letters to Marilyn Brown from Captain Natale Figura

that many of my neighbors think it's terrible that they've come into the neighborhood. But I'm glad Fed Ex is there. They spruced up the place. Prior to their coming, we had the old Barrett's plant, which in turn was taken over by Celotex, and a junkyard. Barrett's, Celotex and the junkyard were terrible neighbors. I'm glad Fed Ex is there. Now, whether they prove to be a good neighbor, I don't know. As long as they keep the property up, I'm glad Fed Ex is there. NR: What type of work did your parents do? MB: Well, before they bought the tailor shop, my father worked at the Navy Yard during World War II. It was a temporary job because after the War, they let him go. He did odd jobs when he could get them. He had only a 6th grade education. I remember he wanted to learn how to read blueprints, but he didn't have enough education, so he did odd jobs. When we lived on Reed

Marilyn Brown, 2002

Street, my father worked as a handyman for a long while. Finally, he managed to get a job at Millar Brothers, which used to be across the street from where we lived. It was a meat packing plant. My mother tried to work but she really didn't. She was a housewife. She would sew for different women in the neighborhood. She was an excellent seamstress. My mother graduated from West Philadelphia High School in February of 1928. She was proud that hers was the last graduating class of girls. She had wanted to go to Hampton University, but her father didn't want her to go so far from home. She then applied to Curtis Institute. She wasn't accepted even though she was an excellent pianist. She had auditioned and, you know, I don't know why she was not admitted. Perhaps because she wasn't good enough or perhaps because she was Black. I never knew. That was a sore point in her life that she spoke very little of.

> "I had wanted to be a Spanish teacher with English or History as a minor. I'll never forget this. I remember I went to one of the advisors at Temple and told her that I wanted to be a high school teacher. She told me that they didn't have any Negro high school teachers in Philadelphia."

NR: She was not admitted to what school?

MB: Curtis Institute on Rittenhouse Square—it's the music school, very famous. My father bought the tailor shop on Wharton Street for my mother so that she could stay home and work and take care of us kids. She did tailoring and she mended clothes. By that time, she had stopped sewing for the women in the neighborhood. She did only repairs to clothing.

NR: What year did they buy the tailoring shop?

MB: In 1952.

NR What type of work did your father do in the tailoring shop?

MB: At that time, he was still working for Millar Brothers. Unfortunately, his health was declining and after a year of our moving, he had a series of heart attacks. When he was able, he helped my mother in the shop. They ran it together. I can still remember him tagging and sorting clothes, when he was able, but a lot of times he wasn't well. My mother took really good care of my father during his illness. He died 10 years later in 1963. The doctors said if it were not for his good care, he would not have lived that long. All of us kids were in high school or junior high school by that time.

NR: Did you help out in the tailoring shop?

MB: Well, I didn't do too much. Occasionally, I would help customers. I would help tag, but it just wasn't my thing. I mean, some of those clothes that would come in! God, can you imagine? You don't realize how filthy people are until you get their clothes.

NR: Did your brothers and sisters help in the shop?

MB: My sister Cissy—because she could sew—helped my mother. Basically, it was my mother and father who ran the tailor shop. My sister took over as surrogate mother because she did all the cooking and washing. My older brother, Carl, left the house before I actually got to know him. He went to Lincoln University in 1952 for one year, then my father got really sick the next year. Since my parents couldn't afford to keep him at Lincoln, he joined the Air Force. Carl came in at the tail end of the Korean War. He had been trained to be a medic. After he was discharged, he worked for a while at Philadelphia General Hospital in their medical laboratory. He stayed with us for a couple of years more, then he got married. He did return to Lincoln University and graduated in 1966. After graduating from Lincoln, he was employed by the University as their Financial Aid /Recruiting Officer. Part of his job was traveling around the country recruiting for his alma mater.

NR: So your brother and sister never lived in the Forgotten Bottom?

MB: Oh yeah, they lived with us. Cissy, my sister, lived there until she was in her thirties. She worked for Scott Paper for 32 years. Prior to that, she used to work for the All Aluminum Company, which was in the 3700 block of Reed Street. That was her first job. Afterwards, she worked for our Uncle Wilbur who owned a laundromat in North Philadelphia. She worked in the neighborhood. I never did. I had a series of jobs. After I graduated from John Bartram High School in 1956, I was admitted to Temple University at night. I had applied to Tuskeegee and Howard Universities and was accepted. But we were too poor. Can you imagine? We were too poor to send me to a Black college. Temple was right here in the City, and you could attend part-time. I remember one year I was able to attend Temple full-time. The cost was about $800 a year—that was a lot of money back then. I had wanted to be a Spanish teacher with

"I remember sometimes in the summer when it was slow [at the tailoring shop] we would go upstairs and take a nap. The door would be open and people would come in and put their clothes on the counter. Mother knew which clothes belonged to whom. Or they would just write a note and say, 'I left it' and they would just walk out the store."

English or History as a minor. I'll never forget this. I remember I went to one of the advisors at Temple and told her that I wanted to be a high school teacher. She told me that they didn't have any Negro high school teachers in Philadelphia. I will never forget

that. I was just a kid. I was so hurt. It affected me that much—boy, that's a bad memory. Anyway, when I was able to attend full-time again, I changed my major and went into business education. I learned how to type and how to do shorthand so that I would be able to either work in industry or teach. By that time, Philadelphia had Black teachers in the high schools.

NR: So you graduated with what degree?

MB: I graduated with a degree in Business Education. I received my second degree in 1972, a Masters of Science in Education. I immediately began working on my doctoral degree at Temple. I completed all my studies and wrote two drafts when I just got tired of going to school and stopped. I did all but dissertation. So here I am at Community College of Philadelphia. Good ol' Temple U. Temple was good to me.

NR: Do you have any children?

MB: I have no children. I have my dogs.

NR: Were you ever married?

MB: I was never married. I was going to school all the time. I didn't have time to get married. Never was . . . came close, but no, never got married.

NR: What was your favorite food?

Marilyn Brown's niece, Frances J. Fuller-Lamar, of whom she is justly proud. Ms. Fuller-Lamar, Executive Director of Project Interconnection, is pictured with Chairman of the Board Raymond L. Kuniasky and former First Lady Rosalynn Carter at the opening of a 21-unit addition of Phoenix House, a housing development for homeless people with mental illness. Phoenix House was built under the leadership of Ms. Fuller-Lamar, who at the time was Project Director. Here she is being honored for her outstanding work as Project Director.

MB: My favorite food that my mother cooked—naturally, it was cornbread. God, I loved it! I even learned how to bake cornbread because I loved it. Cornbread and great northern beans cooked with ham, leftover from Easter. My mother sometimes cooked the beans with salt pork or fat back. God! And this was a poor person's meal. I didn't know this was a poor person's meal, but it was nutritious. I love ham, until this day. And lemonade. My mother used to make homemade lemonade and biscuits. Every Sunday we had homemade biscuits and lemonade. Now ask me can I make them . . . *no!*

NR: You couldn't cook?

MB: Well, I cook a little. I don't cook anymore because it's only me. So if you don't practice it, you lose it. I eat a lot of Stouffer's frozen foods. I get a lot of my meals from Big George's—soul food home cooking. He's at 52nd and Spruce Streets. And I go to Delilah's, which is not only in the Reading Terminal but also at 30th Street Station.

NR: So you are the only child living in the Forgotten Bottom?

MB: I am the only child living in the Forgotten Bottom. My younger brother, Marvin, lives in North Carolina with his wife Faye. My niece Frances lives in Powder Springs, Georgia, which is about an hour from Atlanta. I'm the only one left up here.

NR: Is the tailoring shop still open?

MB: Oh no, it closed so many years ago. It closed completely in the early '80s, when my mother wasn't able to run it. She had begun closing it down towards the end of the '70s.

NR: Do you remember anything about how the tailoring shop looked? Was it always busy?

MB: Yeah, it was really busy; I even learned how to press clothes. I learned how to fire up that pressing machine and learned you don't put the top down because it'll give clothes a shiny look. You get the steam up from the bottom for a soft non-shiny press and just touch the top of the pressing machine to the clothes. You didn't want to mess up the fibers in them. Some clothes needed a hard press. That's when you'd lock the top lid of the pressing machine to the bottom and give the clothes a lot of steam. That was the one thing that the people liked about my mother—she took care of their clothes. She didn't break the buttons; she always made sure the buttons were pinned over before they were sent out for cleaning. You know, when you go to tailoring shops now they don't do all that stuff—you come back with broken buttons, they don't care. She was very meticulous.

NR: So she did most of the work?

MB: She did most of the work, yeah. She did repairs; you wouldn't believe that there had ever been a hole in your clothes—she did like invisible mending. People really didn't appreciate her skills. We used to argue with her and tell her she didn't charge enough. She was a pushover. People would say, "Oh, I'm going to pay you" and they didn't. So when I go to a tailor shop, I always pay in advance because I

"My mother was a great Southern cook. . . . Oh, good golly Miss Molly! One time, Mother tried to sneak a rabbit on us, and we kept saying, 'Why are these bones so funny looking?' As soon as we found out it was rabbit, we said ewwww."

know what it's like to be stiffed. She had four children that she was taking care of. My father would help her out occasionally, but basically, she did most of the work. My mother used to press the clothes sometimes. My father used to press a little, but it was too much for him because of his heart condition. Yes, my mother learned to press and, of course, I learned how to press. We would employ pressers. I remember Freddy was the one who taught us how to press clothes.

NR: Who is Freddy?

MB: Freddy was the guy my mother hired to do the pressing for us. The clothes were sent out to be cleaned, but they were pressed in the store. Yeah, we didn't have air conditioning back then so you can imagine how hot it got in the store. We had a series of fans, but oh, it got really hot. That pressing machine heated up the entire house. It was hot upstairs and it was hot downstairs. At that time, you could leave your doors open. I remember sometimes in the summer when it was slow, we would go upstairs and take a nap. The door would be open and people would come in and put their

Letters home from Mexico—written by Marilyn Brown to her mother, Frances

clothes on the counter. Mother knew which clothes belonged to whom. Sometimes they would write a note and say, "I left them to be cleaned or repaired by Monday" and they would just walk out of the store. We had a little cash drawer in the counter, but we were never robbed. It was that type of neighborhood. People would come and go; the door was open all day and all night. I remember when we were younger we would sleep outside; nobody had air conditioning back then. We would sleep outside in a chair or whatever. Everybody did this on Reed Street, as well as on Wharton Street.

NR: Both of your grandparents went to school down South and

> "I was the Double Dutch queen. I was a kid during the Second World War. We played hop-scotch in the streets and the girls jumped Double Dutch. I learned to play baseball—everybody played baseball. I even played mumblety-peg."

then moved up North?

MB: My mother's parents moved first to Atlantic City, New Jersey when they came North. They moved to Philadelphia when my mother was four. My mother was born in 1910 and my father was born in 1900. His people had moved from Chestertown, Maryland to Dover, Delaware.

NR: What traditional values did your parents teach you that helped shape your world?

MB: Well, they taught us that education was the most important thing that you can acquire. All of us graduated from high school. Only two of us—my older brother Carl and me—were the only ones that went to college. They taught us education was to be valued. My parents taught us that you had to work for everything you earned. We were never on welfare. Even though

there were times when we needed extra money, we never were on welfare. We were raggedy poor. I can remember going to school with raggedy underwear, raggedy dresses and holes in my shoes. We could not afford to get them soled and my parents could not afford to buy me a new pair of shoes. So I would put cardboard in the shoe to cover the hole. I remember I had a pair of shoes that had a flap—the sole of the shoe had come away from the top. The kids used to laugh at me when I wore those shoes. You know kids are cruel. So it was hard work, honesty, treating people with respect and, of course, again, education. Education was always pounded into our heads since we were little kids. I mentioned in my mother's obituary, well, in her tribute, that she taught us to be kind to animals—to not only be kind to people but also to animals. This was a truth that she knew intuitively. Later psychologists would say that a child learns to treat people kindly by showing kindness to creatures that are dependent on them. Both of them, my mother and father, taught us these things and *those* are lessons that I have never forgotten.

NR: What did you do for fun in your neighborhood?

MB: I was the Double Dutch Queen. I was a kid during the Second World War. We played hopscotch in the streets and the girls guess that if my mother knew what I was doing she would have killed me. We used to throw the knife down into the ground. It was some kid's pocketknife. The blades were thick. We'd pull out the blade and tip the knife over and wherever it landed you would do something with it. I don't quite remember; I used to play it often. I was a tomboy. I played a lot with the boys; however, my best girlfriends were Nietsy and Violetta. They were my good buddies. We did foot races, as my grandmother would

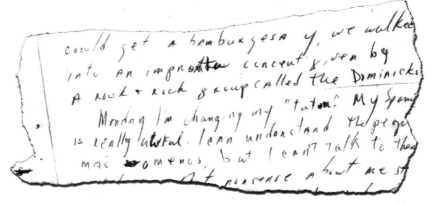

Marilyn Brown's letters home to the Forgotten Bottom from her trip to Mexico in 1964

jumped Double Dutch. I learned to play baseball—everybody played baseball. I even played mumbletypeg.

NR: What's that?

MB: Can you imagine? It was a game we learned to play that had something to do with a knife. I say, "foot rallies." We would run up and down the streets, playing tag, hide and go seek—everybody played those games. We used to go to the playground—they finally built one for us. We used to swing on the swings; I loved doing that.

NR: Where was the playground?

MB: It was . . . this was right before they built the expressway. It ran from Sedgwick Street to 34th Street. We lived at 3441 Reed Street, which really was 35th Street. The playground ran from 34th Street to 35th Street, except 35th Street was where the railroad tracks were. To us it was a huge playground, but now if you think about it, it was only a block. But it was deep. I guess it wasn't that big, but to a little kid it was huge.

NR: But there's no playground there now, right?

MB: No, it was torn up. In the fifties, President Eisenhower and the government were building highways. So Route 76, the Schuylkill Expressway, was built. That was another reason why we moved. The highway was coming. You know, eminent domain. Most of our neighbors had moved by then. There were only a few of us left. We lived beside the railroad track—I forgot to tell you about that.

NR: Where was this?

MB: At 3441 Reed Street. Those big black steam engines. They were coal engines and when they came down the tracks, letting out all that black smoke and soot, you ran to get out of their wake. I remember my mother had finished washing. Do you know what a scrub board is? She would scrub our clothes on the board until her fingers bled. Finally she told my father, "I'm not going to do this anymore." He bought her a brand new wringer

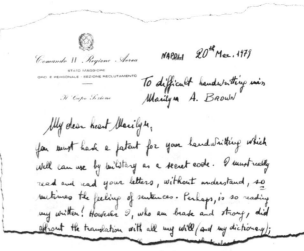

Letters to Marilyn Brown from Captain Natale Figura

washer—that was something. But anyway, we used to wash those sheets on that scrub board—boy, they were nice and white. She would boil them to get them even whiter, then hang them up in the backyard. When we heard the trains coming, we kids would gather up all those sheets and run

Letters home from Marilyn Brown during her visit to Mexico 1964

like hell. We would be covered with soot. It was black and wet! Oh God, those trains! You got used to them, though. That's why nowadays I can sleep with the loudest music on. You know, I don't hear a thing. Yeah, we used to live beside the railroad tracks; we were the last house on Reed Street. Those trains would just shake the entire house. I guess for poor kids—we didn't know we were poor, everybody was poor—we were happy. I could tell you who the rich families were. Of course, Lillian . . . the Gaines, they got the first TV on the block; I think that was in 1949, yeah. Cissy Down The Street (that was her nickname to distinguish her from my sister)—her family got the sec-

ond television set in the neighborhood. We would sit around in the dark watching this tiny screen that couldn't have been any larger than about two or three inches. We would go into Lillian's house, her grandmother's, Mrs. Gaines . . . we would sit around and watch TV. Lillian and her family were the rich ones.

NR: So everyone would go over her house and watch TV?

MB: Those that they invited in, yeah.

NR: So when you were younger, who played amongst each other, like, people of different races?

MB: We were all in our own neighborhoods. When I went to Alcorn [School], I remember my first little white girlfriend was Rosalie Gargano. She lived on Wharton Street in the 3300 block. We were very good friends, I thought. She invited me to lunch one afternoon, and this poor little raggedy black girl—well, at least I was clean—went to her house. I can remember her mother wasn't very friendly. I had lunch there and then afterwards Rosalie and I were not good friends.

NR: Because?

MB: Well, what do you think? Her

mother probably told her that she couldn't play with that little Black girl anymore. I'm sure she didn't express it in those terms. Rosalie was no longer my friend. She basically stopped speaking to me. You know, I didn't understand it at that time. But, as I said, we all went to Alcorn together. But my truest girlfriends were Nietsy and Violetta. They were always my girlfriends—I still keep in touch with them.

NR: Where do they live?

MB: They live in West Philadelphia now, good ol' Nietsy and Violetta.

NR: How did you get to school?

MB: I walked.

NR: High school, also?

MB: No, I took the No. 36 trolley. It used to run on Grays Ferry Avenue at that time. I would take the No. 36 or sometimes the No. 12 trolley. I should've gone to West Philadelphia High School. I didn't understand it then. West Philadelphia High School was closer to me—47th and Walnut Street—but because the School District was very strict about the boundaries, I wasn't permitted to go there. They claimed that we lived within the boundaries of South Philadelphia and Southwest Philadelphia. The School District said I would have to go to Southern, which was predominately an all-Italian school. I didn't want

to go to Southern because most of my friends were going to John Bartram High School. I wanted to go where my friends were. Bartram was a relatively new school. I was only 15 years old. I wanted to attend a newer school as opposed to Southern, which was very old compared to Bartram.

NR: What did you do on Sundays?

MB: We went to Sunday school. We all had to go to Sunday school. Afterwards there was nothing else to do. At that time, Pennsylvania had Blue Laws on the books. Those laws said that all stores were closed on Sundays. My mother didn't let us go to the movies on Sundays, so we listened to biblical stories on the radio. The Greatest Story Ever Told was one of them. We listened to classical music, or we sat around and read. We could play in the streets; we just couldn't play too hard or too loudly. It was Sunday. You couldn't do too much. It was a very quiet day. If you got too loud and boisterous your parents would yell at you. I read a lot. I still do. To this day, I read every night.

NR: Did your mother cook every Sunday?

MB: My mother cooked every Sunday.

NR: What was a typical Sunday meal?

MB: We would have fried chicken —that woman could cook!—potato salad, lettuce, cabbage, sliced tomatoes, kale, greens. I like kale better than greens. That was during the summertime. We only ate what was in season. Every once in awhile, we

funny looking?" As soon as we found out it was rabbit, we said *ewwww*. That was the last time she cooked rabbit for us. It was chicken, either stewed or fried or steamed—they call it "smothered" now. She used to make these giant

Mrs. Frances Azalea Freeman-Brown with her daughter Marilyn (1988) attending her great grandson's third birthday party

would have beef. Usually, it was fried chicken and ham. Ham was mainly for Easter, and sometimes we would have lamb. My mother was a great Southern cook—her mother was from North Carolina, so she learned Southern cooking from her. We had stewed chicken with dumplings, another one of my favorite foods. Oh, good golly Miss Molly! One time, Mother tried to sneak a rabbit on us, and we kept saying, "Why are these bones so

hamburgers and fill them with rice. God, was that good too. Sometimes she would make them with red gravy. I can see them now . . . that big black frying pan with those giant hamburgers . . . it was *good*. Oh yeah . . . those were good times . . . yeah, they were good times— good food. I still love soul food today, as you know. If I could find a good soul food cook, I'd cling to her . . . or him. I know I shouldn't be eating that greasy food—my doctor keeps telling me to stop—but I say, look, it's the only enjoyment in life. Yeah, so clog up those arteries!

NR: What church did you attend on Sundays?

MB: When we were growing up we went to a Baptist Sunday school; I can't remember its name. Nietsy, Violetta and I went. It was their grandmother's church. Sometimes we went over to Mount Zion on Woodland Avenue around 49th Street. My church was Tindley Temple. My mother and father were married there. My mother grew up in Tindley. My grandfather, on my father's side, was a Methodist minister and farmer in Dover, Delaware. When my father came to Philadelphia, he attended Tindley. When I go to church, I still go to Tindley.

NR: Where is that?

MB: It's at Broad and . . . Fitzwater. You *see* how often I go now—I had to think, "Where's Tindley Temple?" We *are* good Methodists. My mother's parents and my family attended Tindley. It's the family church.

NR: What are your treasured possessions?

MB: My dogs . . . I have two Rottweilers. I've had dogs since I was nine years old, although my first pets were cats. When I was nine, my crazy aunt, my mother's youngest sister, gave us a puppy. We thought the puppy was a male, and we named the dog Billy after my aunt's boyfriend. When Billy had puppies, that's when we found out that Billy was not a male. Dogs are my favorite animals. As you can see, I have doggie pictures all over this office. [The interview was conducted at Community College in Marilyn Brown's office.]

NR: Anything else about the neighborhood that you might want to add?

MB: Well, like I said, it is safe. It's

Letters home from Marilyn Brown during her visit to Mexico 1964 not as clean as it used to be, especially Harmony Street. The 1200 block of Harmony Street, and 35th Street are not clean. The people are still friendly. As of now I am the senior citizen—I guess I'm taking over the old guard. There are not too many older people who are left. There are some who are older than me, but most of them have moved or died. There have been lots of changes. Where Bessie's Chicken Shack is, that used to be a bakery. There was an abattoir—boy, did that stink!—on Grays Ferry Avenue where animals were slaughtered. Oscar Meyer was there. Dupont's has been there forever and Fed Ex is now where Barrett's used to be. What did Barrett's make besides a bunch of stinky smoke? I think they manufactured asbestos, I can't remember what they made. We had little grocery shops. There was a butcher shop that was across the street from us. One evening the butcher shop was burned down. No one ever knew the cause of the fire. We didn't have supermarkets so everyone went to different places for groceries and meats. At one time I could name the different cuts of meats, but ask me now . . . everything is in cellophane . . . what is it, Saran Wrap? You would ask for your different cuts and the butcher would cut them for you. But, you know, neighborhoods change and people change. We have gaps where houses used to be. All of my Italian neighbors are gone. My neighbors now are all Black. I don't think we have any white neighbors on Wharton Street or Harmony Street—there are a few left on Grove Street. I think there are two white families left on Grove Street. On 36th Street there is a mixture of

Geneva Brown-Coward and her niece Audrey Azaelia Brown-Fuller

whites and Asians. The same mixes of people are on Sears, Earp, and Reed Streets. We have many Asian people moving in. They tend to stay to themselves. I don't think anybody really knows who they are. Some are students, mostly from Penn. Some run those trucks that you see on Penn's and Temple's campuses, and some have fruit stands downtown.

MB: What inspires you to go on?

MB: I enjoy working here for Community College of Philadelphia (CCP); that's what an education does. It gives you freedom. CCP has been excellent to me . . . I can't complain. I've been able to travel. I've been able to go not only to Europe, but also to Canada and Mexico. As long as I am able, I will continue to work. I have the Forgotten Bottom; I enjoy interacting with my neighbors. We would love to get some of our younger neighbors to join the Association. Maybe they will decide to join later. That is it . . . I am just totally an optimist. That is what keeps me going. I am proud of my family members. I have a family full of dentists, lawyers, medical doctors, PhDs (two), nurses, veterinarians (one), ministers and tons of teachers. §

Lena Clarkson-Gaines

Lena Clarkson-Gaines, 2002

L ena Clarkson-Gaines has spent the majority of her life
in the Forgotten Bottom. Both of her parents are
ministers and Lena has developed a ministry of her
own, dedicating much of her time to educating and nurturing
the women and children of her community. She focuses on
women's health-care issues, encouraging women to inform
themselves about health-related issues. She speaks of this work as
her passion and says, "God has given me as a gift." She is especially
committed to helping children. "It is hard for me to see a child
of need and not be able to do something to help that kid." Ms.
Clarkson comes from a long tradition of very strong women and
speaks warmly of her mother, aunts, and grandmothers. Ms.
Clarkson went away to college but returned to the neighborhood
to be a co-parent to her sister's three children.

"ONE WOMAN, ONE HEART":

AN INTERVIEW WITH

LENA CLARKSON-GAINES

BY VALARIE GREENE

VALARIE GREENE: What year were you born?

LENA CLARKSON-GAINES: I was born here in Philadelphia in December of 1963.

VG: Were you born in Grays Ferry?

LC: Yes, I was born in the Grays Ferry area. I believe my mom had me at Philadelphia General Hospital, which is no longer in existence now—it is called PGH, but, yeah, I have been born and raised in the Grays Ferry area all my life, except for the times I went away to college.

VG: So were you born in the Forgotten Bottom?

LC: No, actually I was born in Philadelphia. My family home was originally at 29th Street, on the 1200 block of South 29th Street. All of my relatives live right here in South Philadelphia, stemming from at least 24th and Wharton all the way down to the Bottom. I had relatives literally on every block. My great-grandmother had seven kids. When her kids moved out, many of them wanted to live close by, so they ended up buying property down in the Bottom. My grandmother has bought her home down there and raised my mother and her siblings there. Our family history is very rich and that would be under the name Gaines: we are quite a large family; we pretty much are all still here in South Philadelphia.

VG: Did you go to Catholic School in South Philadelphia?

LC: I have two siblings—a sister and a brother. My sister and I are only eleven months apart, so we both attended Catholic School all our lives—first in elementary at St. Charles Borromeo, then for high school at St. Maria Goretti, which is down at 10th and Moore.

VG: And how was that experience?

LC: Oh, that was beautiful! I know that set the foundation for my education in terms of my desire for more knowledge, my desire to learn, my desire to share with people anything that I would learn. I was always that type of person . . . I wanted to give back all the time, particularly to women and children.

VG: What type of work do your parents do?

LC: Actually, both of my parents are ordained ministers. Both of them are ministry full-time. Prior to that, my dad was a teacher and my mom was a civil servant for the US government. Both of them have retired and now they are full-time ministry. My dad still does work for the school district. He does some light maintenance work there, but he originally started there as a teacher.

VG: Is the school located in the Forgotten Bottom?

LC: No, my dad was working at Edison. My mother's office—the US Office of Employment and Economic Opportunity was the agency that she works for. That particular office dealt with social service issues on the Federal level, and she had to coordinate different programs: feeding programs, housing programs, and things of that nature. She actually traveled a lot during my youth; she went on the road for her job, but that has been twenty something years ago. She is definitely retired now.

VG: Well, how did you feel about your mother traveling while you were at a very young age?

LC: Actually, we were a very organized family. We always knew what was expected of us. Therefore, when mom went away, mom had planned down to the letter: what we were eating, where we were staying, what uniforms we were wearing—everything was always planned ahead of time, so having her away from home was no major issue for us. We knew what was expected of us. When she came back, of course, we were happy, but she always instilled in us that this is how you do it when I am gone or when I am here.

VG: So would you say your mom was a big influence on you?

LC: Oh definitely! She has probably been the biggest influence in terms of how I shaped my character and grew into a woman. My mother is my number one best friend, my number one fan, and she definitely has influenced me. However, that is because she comes from . . . we all come from a long history of very strong women, who have very strong influences over the daughters that they have.

VG: What kind of games did you play as a child?

LC: [laughs] In our early childhood, we played games such as— and this is right down here, down the Bottom, because my grandmother lived in the house where I

Gaines expressing surprise at a family appreciation gathering in her honor

am currently living in—so the little group games that we used to play were something called Kingfish. We would of course play Double Dutch, jump rope. We used to do these little relay races with the boys and we would play little kickball games and dodge ball.

VG: So tell me about your first love.

LC: My first love . . . um, to be perfectly honest with you, I cannot confess to ever having a first love. For me, I mean in terms of tradition and what people think first love are, I don't think I have experienced it. I know there was a gentleman that I loved; I was never in love with him. He was a friend that I met up in college. My friend was very hard edged and he was into things that my parents would never let me be involved in. They are what my parents would call a "thug." I had compassion for this young man, and he was crazier about me than I was about him, but I knew I had a responsibility to uphold the character and traits that my mom instilled in me. Now, I loved the guy but I wasn't in love with him. I just had empathy and compassion for him. But I have never been in love with anybody, so I don't know what that experience is really like.

VG: So do you have any kids?

LC: Yeah, yeah, I have kids, lots of them! I don't have biological children. My sister, who is eleven months older than me, has born three children—17, 11, and now 4. From the time she started having children, I have co-parented them. I So these are still my kids . . . and the neighborhood kids! Some of the neighborhood kids have struggles in their homes and their parents have to go away or are incarcerated or have to enter rehab programs. That is when I have to step in and I take over and try to keep things as nor-

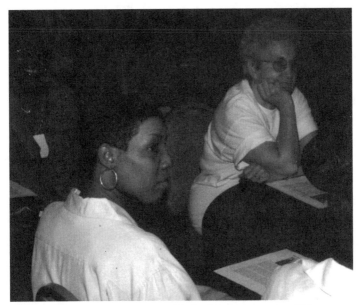

Gaines at a Forgotten Bottom Neighborhood Association meeting, 2002

know from their teachers, doctors, dentists, school uniforms, food, clothing, shelter—you name it, I'm the one who has been there to co-parent the kids. They have a father who is also very active in their lives. However, mothers have a harder time. My sister had to work a lot, full time, so I was the one who supported the children and took care of the children while she was at work. mal as possible until their biological parents get themselves together.

VG: So how do you feel about that?

LC: I love it! For me, that is my passion. That is something I think God has given me as a gift, so it becomes very natural for me. It is hard for me to see a child of need and not being able to do something to help that kid. A lot of times when adults walk by kids, they tend not to notice them. I am fully aware of their presence and their needs and when I see that, I become instantly involved with it. So that is something I really think is a ministry of mine and it doesn't bother me at all. It is the rewards you get from working with young children—how you are able to influence and shape their minds and protect their tender hearts. It is great and I love it.

VG: So besides helping the children, are there any other activities that you are involved in?

LC: I am a church member. I am a member of the Forgotten Bottom Neighborhood Association, where I am the secretary and special events coordinator for that organization. Basically, other than that, I am just more hands on. I am a walking person, a talking person. I'll find out—I'll knock on doors and find out who needs what and how maybe they can be helped.

VG: So how did you learn about the Forgotten Bottom Association?

LC: The Forgotten Bottom Neighborhood Association actually was formulated or came together as a group about five years ago. And that was because of an event that took place where some of the residents were told that some organization or developer was going to come down into our community, which was the Bottom, to buy up the homes and we were going to be displaced. Actually, it was a big stink about nothing. I never thought that was the intention, but it did spark a lot of concern amongst the residents. So we ended up having a meeting. They had quieted down the people to let them

Children playing in the Forgotten Bottom, 2002

know that nobody was coming in to take their homes and at that time we realized that we needed to organize as a group of residents. Most people don't know that there is life down in the Bottom. They think it is all industry, but it is not. So we decided that we needed to

". . . One day a conversation took place between Mrs. Brown, Mrs. Hudson and my Auntie. They said, 'The Bottom don't care about us. They forgot all about us.' And then my aunt said, 'That is what we should call this neighborhood—the Forgotten Bottom.' And then we all agreed that we were the Forgotten Bottom, and that is how we got the name."

get together and organize some type of association and start addressing some of the issues and the problems that have happened in our community. We wanted to do things to better the community.

VG: And what were some of the issues that were of concern in the community?

LC: We have things such as the quality of life issues such as too much trash. People come down and unload big dump trucks in our neighborhood, thinking that it is just a dumping ground. We have a lot of light industrial business down there. We have no recreation for our youth whatsoever. We have some homes that are in desperate need of repair. There is a high unemployment rate amongst our teens. There are many things that we just ignored for awhile, but we are on a ball now. We have been at it for five years now and at this point, it is my agenda to get more young people involved with the association. We have members who have been here for five years, but there are more elderly that can't do the work that is necessary or gather the information needed to really operate this association. So I have recently made it my goal to go after and recruit the younger people that live in the community.

> "Now Mama operated right there on Reed Street, across that silver footbridge that runs across the tracks. Mama had set up a restaurant-style speakeasy, if you will call it. If a person said, 'such and such lost their job,' Mama said, 'tell her to come here.'"

VG: With the name "the Forgotten Bottom," do you think that this particular neighborhood has been forgotten?

LC: Actually, that particular topic came from a direct result of the racial tension that was going on in Grays Ferry. Grays Ferry was experiencing some serious racial problems back down in the area where I said I had grown up at—down 29th Street. We had different organizations, both white and black, forming to try to combat this uprising of racial tension. And those groups couldn't get themselves together and they were protesting and rioting against one another. So actually, my auntie Lillian Ray decided to form a group called Grays Ferry Unified, where we will include every single organization that's in Grays Ferry.

We wanted to all come together under one umbrella and address the issues that are affecting each organization. We started meeting and people came out to these meetings. Both Marilyn Brown and Mrs. Hudson and I continued to go to these Grays Ferry Unified committees and one day a conversation took place between Mrs. Brown, Mrs. Hudson and my Auntie. They said, "The Bottom don't care about us. They forgot all about us." And then my aunt said, "That is what we should call this neighborhood— the Forgotten Bottom." And then we all agreed that we were the Forgotten Bottom, and that is how we got the name.

VG: Today, do you still feel that this neighborhood is the Forgotten Bottom?

LC: I like the name because it is catchy. But no, I don't believe that it is as forgotten as it was five years ago. People have lived down here for years and people have great memories. There is rich, rich history—it could never be forgotten. "Forgotten" in terms of, yeah, we don't receive the city services that we should have like other neighborhoods. "Forgotten" as far as we need recreation facilities, pavements and stuff like that. Yeah, we have been forgotten, but I think that is all changing because of our neighborhood association. We are addressing these issues and we are in contact with the city officials and social services agencies. We are at least now on what I would call the political map.

VG: So do you think that the Forgotten Bottom has changed a whole lot, since you were young?

LC: Actually, no. I do not see much change. When we were younger, most of the people were working moms and dads who had standards for their kids, who kept their fronts clean, and when one kid done something wrong, you can go chastise that kid without replies from the kids' parents. There were more homeowners at the time and more employed adults in the household. So I see it as a better time, a better

quality of life, and I say, at least 30 years ago, it was a better quality of life. Now it is rather splintered because you do not have as many households where the head of the household is working. You have much more elderly people who have retired and their children have grown and moved away. And you have large populations of renters in the Bottom now. All of those factors can change the quality of life, but as an association, we are working on turning that trend around and becoming a community that is able to offer each other supportive services and encouragement. So anything we can do to help one another, we are trying to take it to that level and renew the spirit of the Bottom. We are a tight community and we all support one another.

VG: So what would you say are some other factors that have changed the community?

LC: Partially, it is the death of matriarchs. Many of the matriarchs have died and maybe their homes were either sold or rented to other people that were not raised down here. Then we have matriarchs and patriarchs that have died and their sons or daughters have taken over their property and they have children and raised their children in there. The age of the head of the household has become increasingly younger.

VG: So what would you say is the traditional value that is missing now, in the present Forgotten Bottom?

LC: I will say this: I am 38 years old—the history of the Bottom is very rich through my family and I lived through and witnessed it. The traditional values would be such as my great-grandmother— Her name is Ada Gaines and we called her "Mama." Now Mama operated right there on Reed Street, across that sil-ver footbridge that runs across the tracks. Mama had set up a restaurant-style speakeasy, if you will call it. If a person said, "such and such lost their job," Mama said, "tell her to come here." Mama would feed him, feed his family, and she passed that down to us. We could not sit by and watch anybody have a need and not address the need. And that is the foundation where everything got started and she instilled that in all six of her children, who instilled it in us, who are the grandchildren and great-grandchildren. My grandmother did the same thing. She would constantly whip open her blinds and everybody would sometimes say, "Miss Ella is so nosy!" But Miss Ella looks out because she was a courageous woman. She would not watch a child get beat down in the streets. She would not watch a child walk past her door in the winter on his way to school and have no hat, no gloves. She would open up the door and say, "Come here, boy. Did you eat this morning? Here, put this hat on your

"My fights were always because of someone else. I would end up fighting because I would take up for another child or another person that is disadvantaged. . . . And I would fight and had no business fighting, didn't know what the fight was about, but I like to see justice."

head." That same spirit and generosity is passed down to me and I am the same way now. I am very in tune to these kids and I am very aware of what they are doing, where they are going, what they need, and I address them as such. They belong to all of us, so there is no fear factor for me. Even the older people—I look out for them. Many of the people down here know each other because we are intergenerational families that have maintained good family values.

VG: So would you say that your grandmother is also an inspiration to you?

LC: Oh sure, absolutely—my great-grandmother, Ada, my mama, Norma, and my grandmother, Ella.

VG: So do you think other families in the neighborhood have the same types of values as your family? Or are there families that didn't have that strong family system?

LC: There were other families who did not have what you would call traditional family values, or children living with both their mother and father. Sure, there was much of what we would call dysfunctional family. But you know what? We learned a long time ago that every family is dysfunctional. I cannot find a functional family [laughs]. I have searched high and low, from

college to halfway across the country; most families have a level of dysfunction. It just depends on the degree of that dysfunction and you do not have to stay in it. Your neighbors are here and they can help you if you are not afraid to open up your heart and allow somebody to help you. Some people are very prideful and they do not want their hurts recognized. Some people carry a lot of shame and they do not want that known. Some people are bull-headed, "I can do it by myself, I can take care of my kids!" These are the types of people that I look to and let them know that they can't do it by themselves. God love you, I love you, and if somebody can help you, let them! Sometimes God's desires are to let people love one another. That is hard to get through in an impoverished neighborhood—it is a real hard concept to get through.

VG: So tell me about your first fight.

LC: My first fight!! What a subject! Why would you bring that up? I have been a fighter all my life, physically and verbally. At this age I think I have anger totally under control but I am a passionate person—very, very passionate. Violence to me is always viewed in my mind as the absolute last resort. I am the type of girl, even as a young girl, I can tolerate being called out my name, I can tolerate you being literally two inches from my face, spitting and cursing at me, but if you make a mistake and physically assault me, I am no longer able to control the situation. I was taught as a little girl, from my great-grand-mother and my grandmother, how to defend myself. They would always say, "Don't stand there and let somebody just hurt you! Do everything you can to diffuse the situation. Try to turn the situation around or get out of there, but if they pursue you, that means they want to hurt you and you have every right to protect yourself. I don't care how big they are or how small they are, you use whatever you have to defend yourself. Don't stand there and let somebody beat you half to death!" So as far as fighting is concerned, I had many. I had plenty in Catholic school as a grade school kid because I couldn't

handle . . . my fights were always because of someone else. I would end up fighting because I would take up for another child or another person that is disadvantaged. So when I opened my mouth, that caused instant conflict because the person that is being the bully is going to say, "I ain't talking to you!" But here they are abusing someone weaker and smaller and I cannot tolerate that. I would always interfere and say, "Hey, the situa-tion isn't that bad. Don't mess with the little girl like that—let her go home. All of this is drama!" I tried to diffuse the situation and if the situation cannot be diffused, there are many of days that I have taken a beat-up child home or I would stop the fight or I had to fight the per-son because the little kid could not fight the person and the aggressor wouldn't stop. And I would fight and had no business fighting, didn't know what the fight was about, but I like to see justice. At this age, I

"Now, when I say 'my ministry,' . . . it is not connected to any organized church. It is a personal ministry that I believe that God has given me. That work is to attend to the needs of women and children. . . . It is called 'One Ministry, One Heart.'"

don't really believe in fighting. I am too old to be fighting anybody, but I know that I am a passionate person. I know that no matter what, I will try to keep the peace at all costs, but I will not let somebody hurt me.

VG: Would you say that you ever got into fights because of interracial relations?

LC: Some of the fighting was a result of being called a "nigger," or they would say to my white friend "nigger lover." Sometimes coming home from Catholic school, trying to get home from 20th and Christian to 29th and Grays Ferry, I would often end up in a fight. My fights in my youth were generally as a result of finding a group of bad apples who needed to prove how tough they were. They were just out of control and would try to initiate any conflict because they were uneducated and bored. They should have been in school! You try to avoid these situations and sometimes you are not going to get out of it. You are going to have to defend yourself—it's just that simple.

VG: Did you even get into fights down in the Bottom?

LC: No. My mother was not going to tolerate their two daughters out there fighting. I think at that time,

all the girls down there came from a household of strong women. And those women always nurtured all of us. We are friends and we will always have disagreements, but we were not out acting like a bunch of animals—we talked about it. We did not get into that "he said she said"—it ain't too much to do down here, so if you find something to do, do it together.

VG: So you say you were part of the administration in your church. Can you talk about that?

LC: When I say the word "ministry," it is most often associated with church. My family church is Consolation Baptist Church and it is here in South Philadelphia. It is a couple of blocks down at 25th and Wharton. The pastor there—his name is Alton Gaines and he is actually my uncle. I never called him by Pastor Gaines—I always address him as "uncle." He is my mother's brother. Now, even then in the early years, we had to go to church every single Sunday. Not only did I go to my Baptist church, but I had to go to mass because that was required in Catholic school. We went to church all day on Sunday. Now, when I say "my ministry," I am talking about my ministry from an adult point of view. It is not connected to any organized church; it is a ministry that I believe God has given me to do. That work is to attend to the needs of women and children. I focus on their spiritual, emotional, and their financial needs, such as housing, shelter and counseling. It is a personal ministry that I believe that God has given me. I actually have a name of the ministry. It is called "One Ministry, One Heart." The logo is the number "1" with the word "woman" written beside it. The second line of the logo is the words "1 heart." The logo represents that I am one woman and I have one heart. That speaks volumes to the fact that one person can do a lot to change a little part of the world. I am a woman trying to reach other women, trying to win a heart. It is a way of life for me—this is what I do and it comes natural to me. This is who I am and it is still a ministry. We are all ministers in one way or another.

VG: So talk about the church that you are involved with.

LC: Consolation Baptist Church— wow, what great memories! In the earlier days, we were a mama and papa house church. We had one little row-home house. Actually, it was my uncle and aunt's house. And they had children—they had six children and my mother had three.

We were as tight as can be and still are. We used to have church down in the living room on Sunday. Then the big deal was we bought a property, which meant they bought a row home, around the corner. That was big deal time stuff! Well, when they went to settlement, we marched on around there and we were happy that we had a place to put the name "Consolation Baptist Church" over the door. We praised the Lord up in that church and families came in from the neighborhood to join in. It was so much love. Our pastor, my uncle Reverend Gaines, had an uncanny ability to get people to see their need for Christ. He was able to get people to see that it is about relationship and not church. He instilled faith in the families that came in and he instilled it in us, the young people. So we had a youth ministry, where we washed cars on Saturdays and we had retreats. And each year as we matured and new families came in, we had to move to a bigger building. Finally, we got to our location where we are now in South Philadelphia. We purchased an old supermarket—I believe that it was an Acme. We purchased that building and we have been in the church for about 10 years now. People

In the background: Map of Forgotten Bottom neighborhood from the Atlas of the City of Philadelphia 1910

come and people go, but the funny thing about it is that it is called "the hospital church." We refer to it as the hospital church because when people come in, many people are broken and they are hurt. No matter what condition they are in, my uncle and his staff is able to minister to the souls of these people. And he is able to minister to their needs—if they need a reference or a place to stay, they would have a place right here in the church. It is a church set up to receive a broken heart and to help them on their path.

VG: So what about the interracial business that goes on outside the Forgotten Bottom?

LC: That I know very well because I lived through all of that in the early '70s. Now, none of this took place down the Bottom. A lot of this took place on the block that my family lived in—the 1200 block of South 29th Street. The 1300 and 1400 block and the 1500 block were the dividing lines. Blacks were on one side and whites lived on the other. When I say "dividing line," I literally mean one side of the street versus the other side of the street. Back then in the '70s, I did not know how it got started, but I believe it came from the white people of Irish descent, mainly the

Polish. They had occupied that part of space for so long and had the beautiful homes and they were not having black people moving into their neighborhood. They thought we were ignorant and thought we were below them. They thought we did not know how to keep up the houses. Eventually, those hostilities grew and grew over the years and we knew that you could not cross to the other side. It was a horrible time, but things are much better now. You can freely walk the streets and there are many black residents now and many homeowners on those very same blocks that are black. It is funny because now all I see are a lot of biracial couples and biracial babies. If you keep pressing forward and organize, things can change and that has been a major change in Grays Ferry. They were determined to keep things segregated and now it is not. You can walk freely anywhere down here in the Grays Ferry neighborhood without any hassle.

VG: So you said your aunt is opening up a new restaurant?

LC: Oh yeah! That is the highlight of my life right now, other than my babies. My auntie had just purchased the building two years ago. She has renovated and poured in so much money in it in terms of

> "The first thing that some of these young women say is, 'Oh, I love him! Oh, I miss him!' They can tell you more about 'him' than they can tell you about themselves and about their own bodies. I have an aunt on my dad's side who always told me, 'Girl, don't go out there and give your stuff to somebody and you don't know what you got!'"

investments. It is absolutely beautiful! It is called Melee's and it is right on the corner of our block. It will be family run and I will be heavily involved in that. My aunt has been a hospitality person all of her life. She loves to entertain and she is the best cook in the world! She is known for her cooking, so this is an opportunity for her. We see that this is going to be a good service and ministry to the people down here. It would be a meeting place where your neighbors and people can come in and socialize. We really see it as being a blessing for the community.

VG: So do you think that the restaurant is only going to serve the people down the Bottom?

LC: Oh no! The word is going to spread so fast. That is Ms. Lillian Ray and everyone knows that she can cook, and a lot of people already

know that because she has been very hospitable all her life. I mean, everyone has tasted her food and everybody remembers.

VG: So what type of food will she make in the restaurant?

LC: She does a really good seafood gumbo. She said she is going to serve fresh fish everyday. We are going to do steaks, french fries, hoagies and things like that.

VG: So tell me how you got involved with health issues—you mentioned that you wanted to educate youth and women about health issues.

LC: Well actually, I was born asthmatic. I actually spent a lot of time in and out of the hospital for asthma. As a little kid, I would look around the hospital and wonder why some kids had an illness more severe than mine. I could not figure out

"Grays Ferry: Bridge to the Past" at 34th and Wharton by Josh Sarantitis, Mural Arts Program

why some kids were all alone while my parents were always around. I used to always ask God, "God, how can you let me have asthma?" As I got older, other illnesses started to come forward. I went from asthma, which was a chronic disorder and it kept me hospitalized, in and out a whole lot. Through the years of growing up I knew that it required strength, patience and proper medical care to stay healthy. When I became an adult, it was something that I was keenly aware of. I can tell when a child was sick, whether it was an emotional or physical thing going on. I felt like I knew how to take care of them—not in some medical way, but to provide comfort for them. When the kids got sick, everybody wanted to come to my house because I gave them medicine and I keep their spirits high. I always had big eyes, big heart, and a curious mind. So I would recognize these things and I was always saying as a young person, "I know what I can do to make things better." I have experienced a lot growing up, and I think God has given me great wisdom.

VG: So what do you feel about some of the other health issues that are being brought up such as AIDS, diabetes and cancer?

LC: Actually, the health issues that I think about are issues that primarily affect women and children. My primary focus right now has been the breast cancer issue or any of the cancers, such as colon, liver, and kidneys. The incidence of cancer death down in the Bottom has been very high. Many of the people have died or have been diagnosed with cancer. My mission is to educate and to say to young women, "Look, you only have one body and you are not going to get another body." The body is housing the real you and the spirit and the soul. If you do not take care of your body, you will not live long enough to do the things that may be calling you to do. You might not enjoy your life to the level that you could have enjoyed it because you are neglecting to find out about your body. I particularly focus on women and their sexuality. The first thing that some of these young women say is, "Oh, I love him! Oh, I miss him!" They can tell you more about "him" than they can tell you about themselves and about their own bodies. I have an aunt on my dad's side who always told me, "Girl, don't go out there and give your stuff to somebody and you don't know what you got!" And for awhile, I didn't know what she meant. I know a lot of teens and women who have four children and still don't know the difference between a yeast infection or some more serious sexually transmitted disease. So many women are ignorant about the details of their body. And as far as other health issues, I find out as much as I could about something that may affect both men and women or the black community. I educate myself and I run and tell everybody, "Did you get a mammogram?" Have you done a breast self-exam?"

VG: Has your life been different down the Bottom growing up as a young, black woman? Do you think there are any differences compared to any of the other women?

LC: I think at this age, life is pretty much the same for everybody. Everybody has a strong need for family, a strong need for love, a strong need for education, and a strong need to be able to provide for themselves and their family. Everybody—no matter of their ethnic, education, and economic background—when you stop and start to listen to the sounds of the world, everybody has a cross to bear. And life is not that difficult as we make it seem. Yes, it gets rough at times but my thing has always been, I am a Christian and I have an absolute solid relationship with Christ—I live that and I breathe that. I know how it is to be around a bunch of white people. I know how it is to live around a bunch of wealthy people, but the bottom line is that it is all the same. It doesn't make nobody any better than the other. It's your perspective and it is what is in your heart, and it is your sense of worth and value. And God said we are all valuable to him. The bottom line is: life is the same for everybody, you just have to press through each challenge and opportunity and find a place of peace.

VG: So where do you see the Forgotten Bottom in five years?

LC: In five years, I hope to see a recreational facility, a baseball field, a miniature football field, some swings and some recreational activities. I hope to see at least one of the homes here that aren't occupied as our actual official site that we operate from our neighborhood association. I hope to see that many of the lots are turned into more useful things other than empty lots. I hope to see more of the renters turning into the homeowners. I hope to have more social programs in place and more programs for the youth and teenagers. We are able to deal with the issues that affect us, work on those issues, and try to move it forward to being more positive. We are really going to pass down whatever we do to the following generation. The Bottom is made up of family generations. So now, the young people need to step up to the plate, and let their voice be heard, put their manpower to work, try to turn this place into someplace that is quite desirable for each generation to inherit. And that is my vision for the Bottom in five years, and I think we will get it done. §

William Elliott on his front porch, 2002

William A. Elliott is one of the oldest members of the Forgotten Bottom community. He was born on April 8, 1911 at 1331 South Warfield Street. At 91 years of age, he has lived through and witnessed many changes in the Forgotten Bottom community. His father was a cement finisher and his mother was a home care provider. Many of the activities William Elliott participated in since he was a child have been through his church. He met his wife and the mother of his four children through a friend of faith. Mr. Elliott worked for the post office for 43 years and is now happily retired in the Forgotten Bottom.

JENNIFER IACOVELLI: I would like to start with asking you what your name is.

WILLIAM ELLIOTT: Well, my name is William A. Elliott.

JI: And how old are you?

WE: Well, I'm 90, but in a few more days I'll be 91.

JI: Oh, really? When's your birthday?

WE: April 8th.

JI: That's great.

WE: Yeah, I'll be 91.

JI: So were you born in this neighborhood?

WE: Right here in this neighborhood, yeah.

JI: Do you still remember the house that you were born in?

WE: Well, I was born in a house at 1331 South Warfield Street, but that whole street was eliminated because of the expressway.

JI: Oh really?

WE: Yeah. Right on the other side of the bridge.

JI: What type of work did your parents do?

WE: My father, he was in construction—he was a cement finisher.

JI: Did your mother work?

WE: My mother, she worked in private families.

JI: Private families? What did she do?

WE: Well, she cooked and, of course, the people that she worked for, they were entertaining a lot, so she participated and helped them.

JI: What values did your parents teach you that helped you to shape your views of the world?

WE: The main thing—my mother, she was a Christian, so she always wanted us to be faithful, truthful, and to love one another.

JI: Did you go to church?

WE: Yeah, I went to church. Of course, she was very active in the church.

JI: Now, "Christian," what does that mean?

WE: Well, actually, being a Christian, it's Christ-like—you follow the principles and the teachings of Christ.

William Elliott and Ed Gora, 2002

JI: Where did you go to school when you were a child?

WE: Well, I went to school not too far from here—34th and Wharton. Of course, it's not in existence now. That school was torn down and they rebuilt a school at 32nd and Dickinson, Alcorn School, near Audenreid. From there I went to the Benson School, 27th and Wharton. That was torn down too.

JI: Did you like school?

WE: I didn't mind going because, well, it was a process of learning.

JI: What did you think you were going to be when you grew up?

WE: Well, basically, I thought I would go to school and I wanted to be a lawyer. But due to the fact that my family wasn't in a position to support it, after I went to Central for two years, I gave it up to go to work.

JI: Where did you have to work after that?

WE: Well, first of all, going to Central, there was a bottling company, New Grape, on Broad Street. I used to pass it every time I went to school, so I had an opportunity to go there. That was my first job. It was just one of those cases where

I just happened to be passing it in that neighborhood and I automatically fell into it.

JI: How old were you when you started working?

WE: I was 15.

JI: What did you do after that when you were older?

WE: Well, I worked in the post office for 43 years.

JI: Wow!

WE: Been retired now for 21 years. I thank God that I was able to work in the post office for 43 years and retire, and then not be in a position whereby I feel that, well, I know a lot of people that retire and then look for another job. Lots of times they have to have a job, but I had always hoped to have worked long enough so that retirement would see me through for the rest of my life.

It's not a whole lot of money, but it's enough to live on. I never wanted to be rich, but I always wanted to be in a position to be able to get what I need and what I wanted. But, as far as being rich is concerned, I never figured I'd be rich by working, anyway. You take any person that you know that's rich—basically, they didn't get it from working.

JI: How do you like retirement?

WE: Well, I'll tell you, after being on the job for so long, after 43 years, it was quite an adjustment to retire. But, after you become adjusted to it, it's nice knowing that you can come and go as you please and do what you want to. [Laughs] When I was working at the post office I had to get up around five o'clock in the morning to be at the

"I never wanted to be rich, but I always wanted to be in a position to be able to get what I need and what I wanted. . . . I never figured I'd be rich by working, anyway. You take any person that you know that's rich—basically, they didn't get it from working."

job by six. Of course, I didn't work too far—it was 19th and Christian—but I had to get up to get myself ready, then wait for

William Elliott was employed as a mail carrier for 43 years

transportation to get me to the job. After getting up so early for so long, I feel that now I can get up when I can and I just enjoy the fact.

JI: What do you do now for fun?

WE: Well, I like music.

JI: What kind of music?

WE: Jazz.

JI: Do you play any instruments?

WE: Well, when I was younger I did. In fact, there was a five-piece combination we assembled and we used to go around playing parties and clubs. I had a nice time doing that.

JI: How old were you when you did that?

WE: I was around 18, 19.

JI: What instrument did you play?

WE: I played piano—it was fun. It was not a matter of me going out, or the idea of making money. It was fun and I appreciated being out with people and being in the groups of people, singing, dancing. Of course, I don't dance, I didn't sing, but my wife did.

JI: Tell me how you met your wife.

WE: Well, that happened in 1931. She was active in the church at 15th and Woodland. And there was another friend that I met up with—it was the mother of Harley Williams, the state representative. Her name was Francis Williams. Every Sunday we used to go to West Philadelphia, 47th and Woodland, and a lot of young people, a lot of ladies, a lot of young men, used to meet there. We would talk and just assemble and somehow or another she mentioned to me, she says, "I have a friend that I would like for you to meet." So I says, OK, and she says, "Next time you come, she says she'll be here." We used to meet at her house. So the next Sunday I went there and she was there so she introduced me to my wife and we got to talking and it just went from one thing to another. We used to go to various churches and she used to sing and do church activities. I used to go from place to place with her and lots of times we used to get together and she used to sing and I used to play. From then on, we became close friends.

JI: Were you allowed to date when you were younger?

WE: Yeah, well, I was 19, and she and I are about the same age.

JI: How long before you got married?

WE: About five years.

JI: Do you remember the attack on Pearl Harbor? Were you in the war?

WE: No, I didn't serve in the war at all—I wasn't drafted and I didn't enlist.

JI: What did you think about it? Would you have wanted to be drafted?

WE: No, I never cared for that kind of activity, although my son—he was in the Navy for 28 years and he retired and became an admiral in the Navy.

JI: How many children do you have?

WE: Four—three girls and one boy. [points to a row of photographs] You can look at "The Gallery." We have a Rhodes scholar in the family and we have a commander in the Navy.

JI: You guys have a lot to be proud of.

WE: Well, I thank God for it. I really do, I thank God for it.

JI: Do you see them a lot?

WE: Yeah, I see them quite often.

JI: Do they all live in the area?

WE: Well, in Jersey. I have a daughter that lives in Delaware and she teaches at William Penn High School. My son—he lives in Cinnaminson, NJ—after he retired from the Navy, he began teaching computers. Then I have a daughter who works for a publishing house in East Windsor, NJ. And then, my other daughter, she worked at Quartermaster at 28th, no 20th and Johnson. She's retired and she lives in West Philadelphia. And I have a grandson, and he's just like a son— he teaches in Media.

JI: Oh, really? How old is your grandson?

WE: He's 45. My son who's the oldest—he's 65.

JI: What would you say is your most treasured possession?

WE: Well, my most treasured possession is the . . . well, after I retired from the post office after 43 years they gave me a citation. I would consider that one of my most treasured possessions. Then, I was honored before for Chaplains, and I value that.

JI: Have you ever been in a fight?

". . . When we first moved here—well, the Italians, they took pride in macaroni and meatballs. They called them tomato pies then, but now they call them pizzas. They used to make the sauce all week and they always prized their particular sauce and compared it to others. When they would make it . . . lots of times they would go house to house and share it. But it was like a family—everybody was concerned about everybody."

WE: Well, close discussions [laughs].

JI: So tell me a little bit about the Forgotten Bottom. Are you involved in anything in the community?

WE: Well, the Forgotten Bottom—of course, there were other organizations before, but I wasn't an active participant. But I would meet with them and I was concerned with other things that were happening. I don't know—somehow or another the Forgotten Bottom came to be more of a concerned organization. I guess maybe because I'm old, but otherwise, the other organizations that I belong to just come and go, that's all.

JI: Do you have a good relationship with the people that live near you?

WE: Well, when we first moved here it was mixed, more so than what it is now—it was like a melting pot. And of course everyone was either Italian, Irish, Jewish, Polish. Everybody just took everybody as a member of the family. It was a very close-knit neighborhood and everybody seems to be concerned about what happens to others. Yeah, when we first moved here—well, the Italians, they took pride in macaroni and meatballs. They called them tomato pies then, but now they call them pizzas. They used to make the sauce all week and they always prized their particular sauce and compared it to others. When they would make it—well, look, lots of times they used to go with whatever they made—lots of times they would go house to house and share it. And they took pride in the way they made theirs as compared to what somebody else made. But it was like a family—everybody was concerned about everybody. And in the morning—I mean, the streets were much cleaner than what they are now—we used to get out in the front, sweep the pavement, the front of the street, and take the trash in and bring it out again on trash day. They didn't let it lay all over the place. And we used to wash the side of the house, the steps, and clean the pavement. Yeah, it was nice. Of course, it's a different type of people moving in now all over. All neighborhoods are changing

William and Merlene Elliott

now. But we took better pride in neighborhoods then.

JI: What do you think about how things have changed so much since you were younger?

WE: Well, all I can say is it's progression—things are changing all over, everything is changing all over the world. And there is nothing you can do but take it and accept it, and try to go along and try to live with it, that's all.

JI: Do you think a lot of the conditions in Philadelphia now have to do with population decline over time? Like, for instance, people moving out into the suburbs and not staying in the city?

WE: Yeah, that had to make a change, it has to make a difference. Because naturally, a lot of the people that are moving out of Philadelphia are moving out for a reason, and sometimes it's a particular reason. And, in some cases I can understand it. Well, I have empathy for some people that have caused them to move because a lot of times it's not necessary, and it's uncalled for, and lots of times it's unfair. Because sometimes I run into situations where the conditions or circumstances are set that I don't feel too comfortable.

JI: Have you ever been in a situation where you have been in a different area, like with the Asians that live here or something? You know what I mean? Did you ever go to a restaurant and—

WE: No, I haven't really run into a situation like that to a degree where it has affected me that way. But I don't know, some people, I don't know—they're not thinking, they're not thinking. Sometimes they have created a mind not flexible and then as a result of that their ideas and their attitudes and their approach affects somebody else. Still, if they were put in that position, in the same position that they made uncomfortable for others, they wouldn't like it either.

JI: What would you like people to know about you, your family, and the area that you live in and grew up in?

WE: Well, the only thing that I can say is that I tried to be a person to be agreeable and livable, and tried to be sensible and practical, as far as living with the people is concerned. But there isn't anything that I can see except that maybe others can see more than I can see about myself. There isn't anything that I wanted to point out to you in particular. Just live and try to get along, and try to be self-supporting as much as possible. §

"Well, the only thing that I can say is that I tried to be a person to be agreeable and livable, and tried to be sensible and practical, as far as living with the people is concerned. Just live and try to get along, and try to be self-supporting as much as possible."

Dorothy Gaskins in front of her house, 2002

Dorothy Gaskins is a lifelong resident of the Philadelphia, but did not move to the Forgotten Bottom until the early 1980s, to be with her sister. Her contributions to the community include being the block captain and helping to organize various neighborhood events. Once a Cub Scout leader, she is very much involved with the children of the neighborhood. Now retired, "Aunt Dot" shares an apartment with her "old man," Reginald Stewart. Reggie, who spent his entire life in the Forgotten Bottom neighborhood among family and friends, works for the city.

"I'M AN ONLY WOMAN":

AN INTERVIEW WITH

DOROTHY GASKINS

BY CHRISTY HOCHRINE

"I don't remember exactly what year it was, but I moved down here and I just got a room with him down these little stairs 'cause really, I'm an only woman."

CHRISTY HOCHRINE: So you said that you weren't born in the neighborhood?

DOROTHY GASKINS: No, I wasn't born in the neighborhood. I came up here in like, '80 to live with my sister and I left. I came back in '84 and I've been here since then, 1984.

CH: Okay, do you work around here?

DG: I don't work at all. I've worked since oh, so long—I'm 52 and I retired in 2000. It was for the state—the Welfare Department.

CH: Where were you originally from?

DG: 23rd and Montrose, not far from here.

CH: Where did you go to school?

DG: Elementary I went to Pierce at 24th and Christian and I went to Audenreid for middle school at 33rd and Dickinson and high school I went to Rock at 8th and Mifflin.

CH: Do you belong to a church?

DG: Yes, I do, at 22nd and Snyder, which I don't often go, but my whole family belongs there.

CH: So you moved up here with your sister—

DG: With my sister, and then after I moved up here with my sister and the children started to grow and started getting older and older so then I moved down here with my landlord. I don't remember exactly what year it was, but I moved down here and I just got a room with him down these little stairs 'cause really, I'm an only woman. So then he rented me this little place 'cause really, this apartment here was for a store, so the bare room and everything is downstairs and then my living room and kitchen is up here. I have a lovely landlord, he's not a slumlord.

CH: So you lived here through the riots in Grays Ferry?

DG: Yes, but they were not . . . the riots and stuff—they do not come

Dorothy Gaskins and Reggie Stewart in front of their apartment, 2002

down here, they did not come across 34th Street at all. That's all down in like, 29th and Tasker, and we don't have riots and stuff down here because everybody gets along fine. All Caucasians, every man, every nationality, we do not—when you see it in the paper that says "in the Grays Ferry area" it does not include from 34th Street on back.

CH: And I know you had a lot to say about the FedEx plant—

DG: Ohhhh— the FedEx did us such a wrong deal! So when we first started having our meetings because the Forgotten Bottom was really like, not even on the CDL—you know, when you go and look at the big map where everybody's located. When we started our meetings, somebody went to a CDL meeting and everybody else had a red dot— we had a little black dot. We were not even known until we started having meetings. Most people don't even know that there's this much property back here. We're like a secluded area, but it's nice.

CH: What kinds of businesses were here before FedEx when you first moved here?

DG: Okay, we had Conrad's, we had a carpet factory, salt business, there was another company over there—you know, you couldn't even tell that it was an industrial area, but then somebody put an Industrial sign on my sister's window. When I got here it was a small industrial area, okay. But before FedEx got here, there wasn't anything really around here. We

> "There's no grocery stores, there's no laundromats, no cleaners—we don't have any of that. Good thing my honey bought me a washer and a dryer 'cause we don't have anything! If you want a soda around here past 6:00 or 7:00, you gotta go all the way to Pathmark."

don't have a store; we have to go all the way to the Pathmark to get something at night.

CH: So all of those businesses have gone out of business?

DG: No, they're still here, but I am saying that we don't even have a store— well, that guy Mack closed his store up right on the corner over there right down Grove Street but we do have like a food store that opens up at 6:00 'til 4:00. There's no grocery stores, there's no laundromats, no cleaners—we don't have any of that. Good thing my honey bought me a washer and a dryer 'cause we don't have anything! If you want a soda around here past

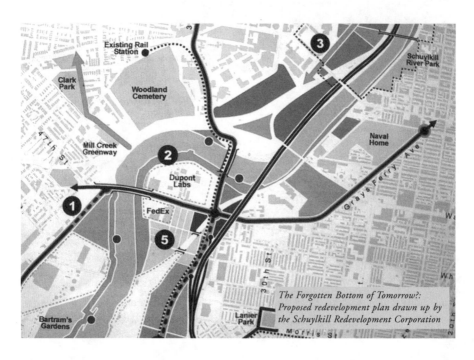

The Forgotten Bottom of Tomorrow?:
Proposed redevelopment plan drawn up by
the Schuylkill Redevelopment Corporation

6:00 or 7:00, you gotta go all the way to Pathmark.

CH: How far is that?

DG: Okay, I'm on 35th Street, Pathmark is 30th and Grays Ferry Avenue. We don't have anything like that but Mrs. Ray is getting ready to open up a store [Mellee's Luncheonette, opening in June 2002].

CH: What happened to all of the jobs that they promised?

Nobody down here is hardly on. Most of them own their own houses, so this is like a community like that. FedEx gave us, like, seven applications, but it was all for drivers. We were supposed to get the other kinds of jobs —after they closed that plant and gave their jobs to their people we were supposed to get the other 72. Not that we had enough people to cover it, you know what I'm saying, but they said

". . . that's when I left the meeting the other day because they're always promising us things that they never fulfill, okay. I say, y'all go on and have your meeting 'cause they gonna open up the river. . . I'm not even interested, I mean, you keep on telling us that you're gonna do something and you don't do it, and it's not right."

DG: Well, Chris, when we first started, they promised us that— Okay, from somewhere they was closing this here plant in another county or whatever—I don't know where exactly it was. They had 100 people to come over here when they had us sign and we agreed to let FedEx come down here— it would boom up down here. They had said some kind of smart stuff like everybody was down here was on welfare.

that we were supposed to get it first. And they did not do that for us, okay. So now whatever we need to do down here, we can do alone because everyone promises us that— They thought that when the government or whoever gave out all that money across 34th Street, they said they gave us something down here. We didn't get a dime, people down here didn't even know about it! That's when we started to have our meetings.

CH: What was the money for?

DG: To do like different little things—improve the community and all that. They did not give us a dime of that money and that's when we started asking about different things, that's when we learned that FedEx was getting ready to come into effect. When they promised us something, okay, and we accepted it, now they want to go down there and do something at the Schuylkill River, okay, and that's when I left the meeting the other day because they're always promising us things that they never fulfill, okay. I say, y'all go on and have your meeting 'cause they gonna open up the river— I have no clue, I had a paper somewhere, I threw it away. I'm not even interested, I mean, you keep on telling us that you're gonna do something and you don't do it, and it's not right.

CH: What do they want to open up the river for? Is it going to be a beach type of thing?

DG: No. I threw it away 'cause I was like, I'm not going to the meeting. 'Cause I was saying, "How y'all gonna sit there, when they already promised us this and that and this— they didn't do that and that's when I left. Not a person around here works at Dupont and not a person around here works at FedEx. Even if they gave our children around here, hey, like a maintenance job— they make good money

A scene from the neighborhood, 2002

and stuff now. We have young people around here that need jobs to keep them out of trouble. They were supposed to open a park for the elderly people that live down here and there's a lot of elderly people around here that would love to have a park to go sit in with benches and all that down here.

We've been down here, well, I haven't been here all that long but I've been long enough to know. And I don't have chick nor child and they come say—'cause everybody calls me Aunt Dot, okay— "When we gonna have a block party?" But if nobody has the initiative to do it, it won't get done. But I don't understand the parents. You are not that busy that you cannot go out there and try to see positive for your children, okay. And the churches need to get involved, you know what I'm saying? We got a church right there and Reverend Jackson, they used to get into things but I don't even see him anymore.

CH: So are there a lot of kids down here?

DG: Oh yeah, we have quite a few kids. Some of them have grown and brought their families down here, then there are families that have gone away and left their houses.

CH: You said that you were block captain. What is that?

DG: Right now I am block captain of two blocks. I clean up the block and I had to be certified to be a block captain. They might come and say that there's a dead animal and I call and have the animal removed. I'm in charge from the Mason's club to 26th Street. I have two blocks; I have no idea why I have them.

CH: So how has the neighborhood changed since you've moved here? Is there a lot of crime down here now?

DG: None. When we started having out meetings and the chief of police came down here and we had our meeting over at the Mason's Club right over there and everybody came 'cause they thought they was gonna take their houses. They came on canes, they came on everything for this, okay, but they just knew that they was gonna take their houses and stuff away. But now even though we had a nice little crowd that day, it was filled up over there. But now it's like they know that they're not gonna lose their houses.

CH: So you said most people own their own homes down here?

DG: Everybody owns their own home and this is where I'm living at right now. Okay, Champ [her landlord] has one . . . two . . . three rooms upstairs and I used to live in the middle room and then me and my old man got to think it was too small. So Champ fixed this up down here for me and this was like a big family that lived down here. You could go that way upstairs, that door over there ... all of this was knocked out and it was a great big house until he made it into rooms. He owns that across the street too. That used to be a store but now it's two small efficiencies and he's got an apartment upstairs. My landlord lives right around the corner on Rose Street so anything that goes wrong—

CH: Have a lot of people been moving out or in?

[*Reggie Stewart, Dot's "old man," joins the conversation*]: Not really. A lot of the houses are empty and just sitting there. The businesses don't stay around long enough to benefit us. We really need them.

CH: Did they talk about that at the meetings too, was it something that they covered?

RS: Oh no, they told us they had representatives. Everyone in the neighborhood had jobs but those companies pulled out of the neighborhood. They tried to talk them into staying and stuff like that. There were quite a bit of factories in the area but you know how Philadelphia lost all the factories and now there's very few factories. Basically, that's the story behind

the violence down here. There was a lot of companies here, a lot of families, jobs went away, and a lot of families went away.

CH: So you said that a lot of your family lives down here?

DG: Well, I am originally from 23rd Street, but Reggie's from here and his family is my family.

RS: I grew up on 32nd Street, and that's where majority of my family is from.

CH: So has it changed a lot since you have grown up?

RS: Oh , yeah. The family situation has kind of deteriorated. You see, I grew up in this neighborhood and 80% was family oriented. There was at least two or three family members in every family in this neighborhood, like a father, two or three sons and his daughters. You know, a situation like that, where some of the kids have moved away, but majority have stayed. It's now gotten a lot different now—they don't stay, they move out as soon as they grow up.

CH: What did you guys do when you were kids around here?

RS: Well, we played sports quite a bit. A lot of roaming around the neighborhood, just, you know, there's a big field back over there and we used to go there and chase rabbits—things like that. One specific church at 32nd and Reed—Williams Temple Church, they used to have chartered trips for us every summer. The church ran the Boy Scout and Cub Scout chartered trips every summer. They don't have that type of activity anymore. We used to have a lot of summer activities like summer leagues for the kids, like baseball, basketball—

CH: And you played at the school?

RS: Primarily, it was more a recreational thing, it didn't involve school in the summertime. We would go to playgrounds. They would have the leagues. Mostly the baseball leagues would be in the day and basketball would be in the early evening hours. It was always the conflict at 30th and Pattison because you had the white neighborhood on one side of the playground and the projects on the other side of the playground. So it was a battle over the playground. They always had a rough time entering the playground because the whites would be at the playground basically all day and then at certain times the blacks would come in and play and they would try to keep them out. So that was the struggle. The kids would get into fights. It would escalate into more of a big thing, but there would be more

fights than anything else. Every now and again, there might be a big tragedy where somebody got hurt. The park at 32nd Street has always been kind of the meeting area for most of the teenage kids and the young kids.

CH: Were you born down here?

RS: Yeah. My father's family and my mother's family come from around here. Everybody is related to everybody.

CH: And they live down here too?

RS: Yeah, all the families are related in one way or another—it's all intertwined.

CH: What street was your house on when you were growing up?

RS: I grew up on Norton Street and 31st. My grandfather had a barbershop. There used to be just about a shop on every corner.

CH: Was that in the '60s or '70s?

RS: The '60s, '70s, especially on Wharton Street, all the way down. There were hardware stores, variety stores, and little candy stores for kids, hoagie shops.

CH: And they have all been turned into houses?

RS: They've been knocked down, a lot of them, or turned into houses or whatever. See, most of the stores, they were on the corners, so most of the corner houses used to be stores. A lot of them were just knocked down. Most of the changes in the neighborhood happened, I'd say, between 1960 and the 1970s. §

Forgotten Bottom Census Data, 1990 & 2000

TABLE 1: RACE & ETHNICITY

Tract 34	1990			2000			1990-2000 Change		
	BG1	BG2	Total	BG1	BG2	Total	BG1	BG2	Total
Total Population	122	344	466	90	273	363	-32	-71	-103
White	0	128	128	9	79	88	9	-49	-40
Black or African American	122	115	237	81	72	153	-41	-43	-84
Asian	0	101	101	0	121	121	0	20	20
Other*	0	0	0	0	1	1	0	1	1
Hispanic or Latino	0	1	1	0	6	6	0	5	5

*Includes population of two or more races

TABLE 2: AGE DISTRIBUTION

Tract 34	1990			2000			1990-2000 Change		
	BG1	BG2	Total	BG1	BG2	Total	BG1	BG2	Total
Under 18 years	33.6%	23.3%	26.0%	23.3%	16.8%	18.5%	-10.3%	-6.4%	-7.5%
18 to 34 years	23.8%	24.7%	24.5%	15.6%	23.1%	21.2%	-8.2%	-1.6%	-3.3%
35 to 64 years	27.0%	30.2%	29.4%	46.7%	38.5%	40.5%	19.6%	8.2%	11.1%
65+ years	15.6%	21.8%	20.2%	14.4%	21.6%	19.8%	-1.1%	-0.2%	-0.3%

Median age in 2000:
41.8 years 42.8 years

TABLE 3: HOUSEHOLDS

Tract 34	1990			2000			1990-2000 Change		
	BG1	BG2	Total	BG1	BG2	Total	BG1	BG2	Total
Total Households	43	137	180	37	125	162	-6	-12	-18

Average household size in 2000:
2.43   2.18

TABLE4: HOUSING UNITS

Tract 34	1990			2000			1990-2000 Change		
	BG1	BG2	Total	BG1	BG2	Total	BG1	BG2	Total
Total	47	153	200	51	151	202	4	-2	2
Occupied	43	137	180	37	125	162	-6	-12	-18
Owner occupied	22	111	133	17	92	109	-5	-19	-24
Renter occupied	21	26	47	20	33	53	-1	7	6
Vacant	4	16	20	14	26	40	10	10	20
For rent	0	3	3	3	16	19	3	13	16
For sale only	0	3	3	1	3	4	1	0	1
Rented or sold, not occup	0	3	3	2	0	2	2	-3	-1
For seasonal, recreational	0	0	0	0	1	1	0	1	1
For migrant workers	0	0	0	0	0	0	0	0	0
Other vacant	4	7	11	8	6	14	4	-1	3

Census figures from the Schuylkill Redevelopment Corporation

Ed and Joyce Gora

A life-long Forgotten Bottom resident, Edward Gora was born on September 9, 1933, in a home "three doors from the home I'm living at now." Coming from a family of 12, Mr. Gora remembers it being a tight squeeze in their three-bedroom house. He attended grade school at St. Mary's of Czestochowa and went on to West Catholic High. After graduating, Mr. Gora began his working life, taking jobs in an insurance company, an outdoor furniture store, at General Electric, Burrows (which later changed to Unisys), and eventually retiring from Perfect Precision, where he worked as a mechanical inspector. He currently resides on Wharton Street with his wife Joyce. As vice-president of the Forgotten Bottom Neighborhood Association, Mr. Gora stays actively involved in the community.

"ONE BIG HAPPY FAMILY":

AN INTERVIEW WITH ED
AND JOYCE GORA
BY JESSICA MALEY

JESSICA MALEY: I figure the best place to begin is to start out with when you were born and where.

EDWARD GORA: I was born Sept 9, 1933. I was born in a home three doors from the home I'm living at now.

JM: You were born inside your house?

EG: As far as I know, yes.

JM: Did a midwife come?

EG: Yes, we had a midwife, yes.

JM: Is that how all of your brothers and sisters were born?

EG: I don't believe so.

JOYCE GORA: I think the last two were born in a hospital.

EG: My youngest brother and sister were born in the hospital. I was the last midwife child.

JM: So you were the last one to be born with the help of a midwife . . . interesting. Was that common for everyone in the area?

EG: I believe so. There was one woman who used to do it. This used to be a Polish neighborhood; we had a Polish school.

JM: So she did the neighborhood also?

EG: Yes, yes she did—

JM: That made it very convenient—

EG: Yes—

JM: You never had to go out.

EG: In fact, she lived in a house right where the club is where we had our meeting [the St. John's Club, where the Forgotten Bottom Neighborhood Association meets]. She lived in that house there.

JM: That's very central.

EG: Yes.

JM:. Where did you go to school?

EG: Well, school, being of Polish descent, my mom and dad sent me to school at St. Mary's of Czestochowa.

JM: St. Mary's what?

EG: St. Mary's of Czestochowa.

JM: How do you spell that?

EG: C-Z—

JG: E-S—

EG: E-S-T-O . . . you got me. [Smiling]

JG: [Laughs] Write it down.

JM: [Handing Ed a notebook] Here, do you want to write it on this?

EG: T-O—

JG: C-Z-E-S-T-O-C-H-O-W-A.

EG: You got it over there?

Czestochowa [which] was a place in Poland, like you would say "from Philadelphia" or, you know, whatever, so it was a place in Poland.

EG: It was a Polish community and we used to have a bus come down and pick all the kids up from the neighborhood as far as 27th and Snyder [Street] and take us to school.

JM: How long was your bus ride?

EG: I guess about a half hour or so.

"[At school] we, the Goras, used to sit on one part of the porch to eat lunch. Why? Because my mom—what she sent for our lunch was a loaf of rye bread and cans of sardines. . . . The kids wouldn't like the smell of it [so] they sat down on the other end."

· ·

JG: Yeah.

EG: [Handing Joyce the notebook] Here, you write it. I'm the Pollack and she has to write it. [Laughs]

JM: What does that mean, Czestochowa?

EG: Well, you got me.

JM: You never learned?

EG: I never . . . never knew.

JG: It's a place in, isn't there a place in Poland? It's . . . St. Mary is from

JM: I see, so it wasn't too long.

EG: No. We had all Polish nuns. The school was all one big building: it was the school, the rectory, and a convent. Some of our classes, like fourth and fifth grade, were in the same room with just a divider between.

JM: Really, so could you hear the teacher on the other side?

EG: Yeah, just about.

JM: Wasn't that pretty distracting?

EG: Yes, it was. When I went to school, there were five of us that went to school at the same time. We used to eat lunch out on the porch. We, the Goras, used to sit on one part of the porch to eat lunch. Why? Because my mom—what she sent for our lunch was a loaf of rye bread and cans of sardines.

JM: That was your lunch?

EG: That was our lunch. We'd sit there with our cans of sardines and rye bread. The kids wouldn't like the smell of it [so] they sat down on the other end.

the school was in went home for lunch.

JM: How long did you have to eat your lunch?

EG: An hour. We had a playground out there so we could go out and play.

JM: That was a nice long break.

EG: Well . . . that meant that the nuns got to have their hour too.

JM: So you went to school with five of your brothers and sisters, but how many did you have all together?

EG: I come from a family of twelve—seven brothers and five sisters—

> "I come from a family of twelve—seven brothers and five sisters. We used to sleep three to a bed . . . "

JM: Would you eat that every day?

EG: Oh no, it wasn't every day, just certain days—

JM: Right, but enough so that the kids knew to stay away?

EG: Yes.

JM: That's pretty funny. Did everyone pack a lunch? Was there a cafeteria?

EG: No, we didn't have a cafeteria. The kids from the neighborhood

JG: Six brothers, you were the seventh. Oh, he had one, he had two brothers: one was killed in the service—

EG: One was killed in the service, Michael, and my other brother Frankie died when he was six months old.

JM: Still, there were twelve of you?

JG: Yes, and in a three-bedroom house.

JM: There were only three bedrooms?

EG: Three bedrooms, yes. We used to sleep three to a bed—three bedrooms—and one had two beds in it.

JM: Were your parents in one bedroom, and the other bedrooms split between the girls and boys?

EG: No, it was me, my father, and my brother, but just on weekends.

JM: That's definitely a tight squeeze.

EG: Yes.

JM: Can you think of anything fun that would come out of this living arrangement?

EG: There was always someone to beat up on [laughs].

JM: Would you and your brothers and sisters get in fights a lot?

Ed Gora and friend

My father worked nights so it was good. While he was working, we'd have the bed. When he was home, me and my other brother would sleep with him in one bed. Two girls would sleep with mom, two girls would be in another bed, [but] we found room for everyone. It was a little crowded—

JM: So you were rearranging all the time?

EG: Yes.

EG: No, it was just typical childhood stuff, but no real fights.

JM: So you and your siblings got along pretty well?

EG: Oh yes, and we still do.

JM: You had told me before that you were the only one of your siblings who remained in the neighborhood, right?

EG: Yes, all of my brothers and sisters moved out, to other parts of the state or New Jersey. I'm the only one who decided to stay here. We got married in '55, moved out for about four years, and then came back. The community here is like one big happy family. Everybody knows everybody; whites and blacks—we all get along good. As children, if my mom ever wanted me, I was down at some black people's house, the Scott's, and the same thing if they'd be at our house. It was one big happy family.

JM: If your mom needed you, how would she get ahold of you?

EG: Well, we knew if it was suppertime or dinnertime or something like that . . . we knew we had to be home at that time. We better be home, so we adjusted ourselves to be home at that time.

JM: What would happen if you were late?

EG: We'd get our scoldings, a few times we got beatings, which you're not allowed to do now because children can divorce their parents today. We used to get spanked.

JM: So you knew better.

EG: We knew better, right. Mom wasn't as strict as dad. If I had done anything wrong in school, nuns smack me on my knuckles, I'd be afraid to go home and tell Mom because they'd double it. They'd say, "Well, the nun has reasons . . . they hit you for some reason, so you must have been bad." I'd get a few more whacks on top of it so it was best just to keep your mouth shut if you had been bad in school.

JM: Right, because they always doubled the punishment.

EG: Oh yes.

JM: Was your school very strict?

EG: Yes. We didn't have to wear uniforms, but we had to wear white shirts, dark pants, and a tie—it had to be no dungarees, no sneakers.

JM: Was it common for someone to get hit by a ruler?

EG: No, just if you deserved it.

JM: Do you have any special mem-

· ·

"We'd all crowd at the gate—there'd be five or six of us—and we'd see a guy coming out of the building—'Hey Mister! Mister!'—and we'd be pushing each other trying to get the guy to get us to run to the store just to get some extra pennies."

· ·

ories from being a kid in the Forgotten Bottom?

JG: They used to have a train running from here to Atlantic City that the companies in the area would donate and you'd go down on the train for a day.

EG: They'd give us ice cream. Even the adults would have ice cream too. It was a good day out, at least one trip a year. It was just the community spending time together. When Barrett's was here as a kid—we used to have two or three deli stores—we'd stand by the gates and run errands and go to the store for these guys. They'd get us to go to the store for them to get them a sandwich and they'd give us an extra nickel or dime. We'd all crowd at the gate—there'd be five or six of us—and we'd see a guy coming out of the building—"Hey Mister! Mister!"—and we'd be pushing each other trying to get the guy to get us to run to the store just to get some extra pennies. Another thing we used to do is go around and collect milk bottles. We used to get a penny or two cents on a milk bottle—same thing with soda bottles.

JG: Money was tight then with twelve kids.

EG: Yeah, those were the good old days. We'd go to the movies for eleven cents. On Saturday when you'd go in they'd give you an envelope with a couple a pennies or another movie ticket. We'd get a couple of pennies and go in there and put them in the peanut machine right away.

JM: What kind of movies would you go see?

EG: At that time [there were a lot of] cowboy and Indian [movies], Shirley Temple, or war movies.

JG: They used to have dish night for the ladies, like on a Wednesday night if you went to the movies you'd get a free dish. In those days when they showed movies they used to show scenes from the war. It was the news before the movies.

JM: Did you have a favorite?

EG: Well, I like movies with Gabby Hayes, Roy Rogers, and Gene Autry—those were the good days. Now you turn the television on and all you hear is cussin', you can't even watch it. Years ago we used to sleep outside on the front sidewalk during the summertime and nobody bothered us.

JG: We still sit out there.

EG: Oh yeah, we sit out there.

JG: The door's never locked until we go to bed at night. That's why we said we don't really want anyone to know we're here. It's there on the map, but they don't notice us because we're so small. It's such a

Ed and Joyce Gora with neighborhood residents William Elliott and Romeo Rivello, 2002

small community that you just overlook it.

JM: Was there anything particularly special that happened here on holidays?

EG: As a kid around Easter we used to go around with a hard boiled egg and try to crack each other's egg. Whoever's egg would break would have to hand their egg over to the other person and we'd see who got the most eggs. The other day I just heard someone call up a radio station when the guy was asking about Easter traditions and he talked about the same thing, he called it "Aper." I would hold my egg pointy side up and the other kid would hold his pointy side down. If my egg broke, I lost and he kept the egg. We came home with many eggs—we'd make egg salad or just eat the hard-boiled eggs.

JM: After grade school where did you go?

EG: I went to West Catholic High on 49th and Chestnut. The first year, as a freshman we had a West Catholic Annex at St. Mary's because West Catholic was so crowded.

JG: That must have been a big change to go from that little school to a big school.

EG: It was a big change. At St. Mary's we were in one class all day—there was no changing classes, we were in that one room all day, whereas in high school we had to run the halls after every 45-minute period. We had five minutes to go up to the third floor and down.

> *"I guess this was in '53. . . . I had lunch and then came out of lunch to see my buddy standing there with his arm up getting sworn in. It was funny it worked out that way because I talked him into it when he hadn't really wanted to go. Here he was being inducted and I hadn't gotten in."*

··

There were "up" stairs and "down" stairs. You couldn't come down the "up" stairs.

JM: What did you do after graduation?

EG: After graduation I went out trying to look for a job. The one job I got was at a clothing manufacturer where I spent a couple of months. Then I went working for an insurance company. It was me and my buddy.

JM: Were you selling insurance?

EG: No, we were working at an insurance company using IBM machines. They started me and my buddy on the simpler machines. This outfit was run by Jewish people who, well, any new help after us that were of Jewish descent got the boost over us—

JM: They got priority.

EG: Yes, and we were just sitting there. So I talked to my buddy and said, "Let's go enlist in the service." So, we went up and enlisted.

JM: What year would this have been?

EG: I guess this was in '53. We got up and enlisted, and then went up for our physical but I had a collapsed lung. At that time you would have your physical and would get right inducted into the service. When I went in they questioned me about my health and I told them about my collapsed lung, which at that time they rejected me for. I had lunch and then came out of lunch to see my buddy standing there with his arm up getting sworn in. It was funny it worked out that way because I talked him into it when he hadn't really wanted to go. Here he was being inducted and I hadn't gotten in.

JM: He got enlisted but you didn't and you were the instigator.

EG: I was the instigator.

JM: How did you get your collapsed lung?

EG: Well, to tell you the truth, I

worked for a factory right around the corner that made outdoor furniture. It was a hot day and I just wanted to go home—I wanted the day off. I told my boss that I didn't feel good. He said, "If you don't feel good, we'll take you to the hospital." I got to the hospital, [and] they gave me the X-rays and found I had a collapsed lung and I didn't even know it. I had used the excuse I was sick just to get out of work and here there was really something wrong with me.

JM: Not only was it a surprise, but you also were able to prove to your manager you really were sick. Here you thought you were just trying to get out of working that day. [Laughter]

EG: Then I had some bad instances. I had a back injury, two discs removed, double hernias—

JG: Another collapsed lung, but that was a bad one.

EG: After they found out I had the ulcers they told me to stop smoking; otherwise, I'd be back again in

six months, but in six months I was back again with a perforated ulcer. After that ulcer I had my second collapsed lung and they fixed me up some. They had to cut all the way from the front of my chest to my back; it was quite painful. So I had

Inside the St. John's Club, 1314 S. 36th St.

two close calls, but I still smoke. Even when I was in the hospital I smoked—at that time you were allowed to smoke in hospitals—so here I was smoking and the doctor walked in. The doctor grabbed the cigarette from me and took the pack that was sitting there and said, "Here I go and save your life and you sit here smoking." What he didn't know is that I had another pack in the drawer. I've always been a smoker and I just can't seem to stop. I'd like to stop, but I don't think I could.

JM: How old were you when you started smoking?

EG: It was probably in grade school.

JM: It wasn't something that your parents minded?

EG: Well, everything was on the sneak. They weren't happy about it. My dad was a heavy smoker but I'm not blaming him. None of my

JG: Don't make excuses.

JM: How do you feel about if your kids or your grandchildren would smoke?

EG: I'd like to twist their necks. My one son, my oldest son, he started smoking in his thirties. He picked up a cigarette and started smoking. I tried to stop him but I guess he's following in his father's footsteps.

A meeting of the Forgotten Bottom Neighborhood Association, 2002

brothers smoked, I was the only one.

JG: Well, your brother Joe smoked, but he quit. Steve smoked, but he quit.

EG: Yeah, they both quit early. I was the only one.

JM: So you felt you had to carry on for your dad?

EG: [Laughs] Yes.

JM: After your friend enlisted, what did you do instead?

EG: That's when I worked at the furniture place. At that time I was making $1.85 an hour. It was piece-work. The rates were so tight that if I made $2 an hour we were making big money. After that I got a job at General Electric. I started as a jani-tor for about two months. The first day I was there my boss caught me playing pinochle. The boss didn't say anything to us. He always said, "If you get your work done I don't care what you do." I had a room about as big as this house and my job was to empty the wastebaskets and do the dusting and that's all I had to do—

JG: For about two months and then he went to inspection—

EG: Then I went to into the stock room and that lasted about three months. Then I got my break and became a mechanical inspector. I was there when I had my back surgery in '65. I was supposed to get laid off. I was done with my leave of absence for my surgery and was supposed to go back but I knew there were big layoffs and if I went back I'd get laid off. I talked to the doctor to extend my leave of absence and he extended it for two more months. The day that I did go back they laid me off, but by that time I had my ten years and was able to get a pension.

JG: Then you went to Burrows.

EG: At General Electric I worked in the missile division. Then I went to Burrows, which was an accounting business. I worked there as a mechanical inspector. I got laid off from Burrows when it changed to Unisys and went to Perfect

Precision and worked as a mechanical inspector until I retired. Now my job is to clean the house and wash the dishes [laughs].

JM: As kids, what would you do for fun?

EG: A lot of times we'd play marbles or "Cowboys and Indians." Or we'd go swimming up on 49th Street where they had hour swims. At that time if you were in from say 1:00 to 2:00 they'd make everyone get out and you couldn't get back in if your bathing suits were wet. They'd feel your suit and if it was wet they wouldn't let you in. What we'd do is carry two bathing suits and while we were swimming let the wet ones dry. That way we could stay three hours or so.

JM: Why did they only let you swim for an hour?

EG: Because it was too crowded.

JM: But you found a way to work around it.

EG: [Laughs] There was a whole gang of us that used to do it, but we learned it off the elders.

JG: Oh, the elders taught you how to do that.

JM: Was it free to swim there?

EG: Yes.

JM: Did you play down by the river?

EG: Oh yes, we used to walk along the banks looking for balls. They used to have a field upstream with tennis courts. Lost balls would end up in the stream and that's how we'd get our tennis balls or baseballs.

JG: [Did you] fish?

EG: Well, we did some fishing down there. That time as a kid we didn't have fishing rods. We'd find somebody throwing an old screen away, put strings on the four corners, put a stone at the bottom of the screen and throw it down to the bottom and pull it straight up. We'd catch some catfish that way.

JG: At that time the water was clean.

JM: Oh, the water was clean at that time.

EG: Yes.

JM: Did you ever eat the fish you caught?

EG: Oh no. It was just something fun to do. Now they do a lot of fishing, a lot of people go right down the street behind FedEx with fishing rods and they spend a couple hours there. We haven't been down there for awhile. Some of these Black people eat them. We see them walking up the street carrying the fish with them.

JM: Now that you're retired I know that you have a job sort of watching out for the neighborhood.

JG: She's talking about your radio.

EG: Oh, my CB. My wife had bought me one about ten years ago and that's all I listen to. If I hear anything on it during the day I'll be

A graffiti writer says "Amen," 2002

"They used to have maps of the city with pins in troubled areas and there were no pins on this neighborhood. I was told by a policeman that they were told not to bother coming down here because nothing happens."

the first one out there before the police get there—or there before the firemen come down.

JM: Has anything happened recently?

EG: Just recently, someone was shot in a different neighborhood but they dropped the body off two streets down from here. This neighborhood is quiet. If anything happens, somebody steals a car, they drop it off here. If they have dogs, they drop stray dogs down here. As far as any kinds of robberies or thefts, we don't have none. If there is something, people find out. We as a community all look out for each other. Everybody knows each other. As a kid, if somebody seen me doin' something it would get back to my mom. If anything goes on now, if somebody comes in and they do something, we come back and tell them we don't do it that way and they make the change. There were some people who lived here for about six months—it was like Grand Central Station—people

used to run in and out all the time. We talked to them, and I guess they decided to move out.

JM: It must help that the neighborhood has such open communication.

EG: If anything goes wrong we all talk about it. If you see anything, if you see any kids doing anything, we say something. That's the way we all get along.

JM: Do you think the reason this area is used to dropped off stray dogs or stolen cars is because people know this neighborhood is so quiet?

EG: It could be. When we first started this community project we invited the cops down and the captain came and didn't even know this area existed.

JG: He was the police captain.

EG: He didn't even know about us. They used to have maps of the city with pins in troubled areas and there were no pins on this neighborhood. I was told by a policeman that they were told not to bother coming down here because nothing happens. Some people fuss about that, like with what happened the other day with the person who was shot being dropped off. They say, "We need more cops in the neighborhood." Well, me with my CB, I know there are police around. They may not be in uniform or patrol cars, but they're around. I see them when I run out and they'll ask me, "Where's your radio?" That day my

with the FedEx coming in, FedEx got together with the Dupont's and they've really helped fix things up where it used to just be old factories. They put in grass and trees and it really looks nice. We had rats as big as cats before, so this is really a big asset to us. The way I understand the Schuylkill River Authority—we had a meeting with them—they tell us [that] they're in the process of redeveloping all along the river with parks, stores, and even riverfront homes. They're supposed to have crosswalks and they even talked about having a performing arts center. They have big hopes for this. This has been going on for years.

Ed and Joyce Gora, 2002

batteries had run out. There are plainclothes men around. I tell those people who complain that if they could listen to my radio they would know that with the troubles around, even just over on 49th Street—we've got nothing compared to that. The only reason the cops would need to come down here is if we'd have those troubles, and we don't want those troubles. Now

JG: They worked all the way up to Market Street. Now in June they're supposed to work from Market Street all the way down to South Street. After they finish up they're supposed to start at South Street down to this way. It's the Schuylkill River Tidal Development something. They've got a lot of plans for everything. The most things we're worried about right now is the higher taxes and more traffic. But that's in the future—that may be in another ten years.

EG: Yes, we may not be around to see that. The main thing is that we pray they keep the community the way it is now. We're afraid that if we get noticed we'll bring in some of the riff raff.

EG: We're considered Grays Ferry here, but Grays Ferry goes all the way to 25th Street. On this side of the highway it's good, but once you get to the other side that's where all the trouble starts.

JG: That's the Grays Ferry you always hear about.

EG: Like that little girl who got raped the other day. Someone will hear something about Grays Ferry and they'll say, "Oh, Grays Ferry, that's where Ed Gora lives." They don't realize that's not here.

JG: We're so far west of all that. We're so far west that all you have to do is go across the bridge and you're in West Philly. They think we're southwest, but we're south.

JM: How long has the name "the Forgotten Bottom" been used for this area?

EG: We were always called The Bottoms—

JM: Why?

EG: We're way down at the bottom. But then different parts of Grays Ferry—

JG: Where they have the trouble—

EG: The city fixed the houses, paved the sidewalks and did different things to make it better. We had been trying to upkeep our area, but we never got help from the city; no pavements, no streets—the streets used to be cobblestones—so we were forgotten.

JG: Yes, so about five years ago we got a group together and have tried to finally get something done down in this neighborhood. We got our streets paved; we're still waiting for sidewalks.

EG: The city has finally recognized us. Our big trouble right now is that the same people that are complaining the most about nothing being done around here are the same people who never show up to our monthly meetings. I put up flyers on all of the telephone poles and slip them under their doors but they still never come. Last year we even threw a street party for the younger generation but it was hard to get people to come.

JG: They want things to be done but they don't want to be bothered doing it. §

James Hudson

James and Selista Hudson

Born in August 1943, Mr. James Hudson has lived his entire life in the Forgotten Bottom. His father worked at a meat company at Front and Venango and his mother was employed at All Aluminum. He attended Bartram High School until the 10th grade when he moved out of his parents' house and began his working life. Presently is happily married to Selista Hudson and working as a security officer at the Independence Building. He is a Deacon of his church and sings for the gospel choir. Mr. Hudson says of the Forgotten Bottom "I'd rather live here than anywhere else."

"I DID MY SHARE OF DEVILMENT":

AN INTERVIEW WITH JAMES HUDSON

BY JENNIFER REILLY

JENNIFER REILLY: What year were you born?

JAMES HUDSON: 1943—August 23, 1943.

JR: Were you born in the Forgotten Bottom?

JH: The Forgotten Bottom all my life—59 years.

JR: What was it like growing up here?

JH: It was nice. We had our share of fun. There was a playground over on 34th and Reed. We used to go there and play. And then we had our share of factories down there, too—Barrett's, All Aluminum, Dupont's. We used to go fishing back there; we used to go back there on Schuylkill Avenue, cross the trestle, and we'd end up in Bartram Village. We had a lot of fun—did our skating and riding our bikes up and down the streets. Mostly, it was quiet down there. Everybody got along. We had a little share of trouble but it wasn't really bad. I would rather live here than anywhere else because it's still like that now, it's still quiet. A lot of new people now I never knew but still we all get along.

JR: So do you feel it changed at all?

JH: I mean, as far as people, and they just put the FedEx over there. All Aluminum is gone now. There's an open lot back there now. And there don't be that many people here now like there used to be. There used to be a bar right there at 36th and Wharton. A lot of harmony—everyone gets along.

JR: What did your parents do for a living?

JH: Well, my father worked for a meat company down at Front and Venago. My mother, she worked back at All Aluminum for awhile. I forget how many years she worked back there; it wasn't that many. Then she got pregnant again and she never went back to work.

JR: What was the highest level of education you received?

JH: 10th grade, then I quit school

> "My father, he took care and provided for the family.
> I was of age . . . so I just took care of myself when I
> was about 17. Ever since then I've been on my own."

and went to work.

JR: Where did you go to work at?

JH: I went to work at the airport—the International Airport.

JR: Was that to help your family out with money?

JH: That was to help me. My father, he took care and provided for the family. I was of age, though, so I just took care of myself. I started taking care of myself when I was about 17. Ever since then I've been on my own.

JR: Did you move out at 17?

JH: I left my mother and father's house and went to stay at my grandfather's house. Stayed there a lot of years. Then he passed, and I stayed there a little while. Then I winded up getting married. It was nice. I didn't have a bad childhood; I really didn't. I had a lot of fun. And as a teenager we had parties down here and block parties and all that.

JR: Were there a good amount of kids your age?

JH: Yeah, a lot of us grew up together down here. A lot of them passed on, some done moved. I don't see them too much no more. I'm about the only one in my crowd still down here, you know, my age. Out of my friends, I'm still the only one down here.

JR: What work do you do now?

JH: What type of work? I'm a security officer.

JR: Where at?

JH: 5th and Walnut, the Independence Building.

JR: So what do you think makes the neighborhood so special?

JH: Because everybody gets along, I think that makes it special. Anywhere you go, if everybody gets along, you can do just about anything. It keeps the peace down here. You can go to your neighbors to get a cup of sugar, things like that. No arguments, no fighting, no jealousy or stuff like that. That makes the neighborhood nice, I think. We don't have no people hanging on the corners or stuff like that. It's not like that down here. It's always been like that, since I can remember. My father said the same thing:

when he was growing up down here, everybody just got along. The white would look out for the black, the black would look out for the white. That's the way it's always been.

JR: Do you have any treasured possessions from growing up?

JH: No, I don't have nothing. Got rid of all that stuff. The house I'm living in now, my aunt used to live in. She lived in here a long time. She was living here, I guess, in the 1930's. She just passed on 7 or 8 years ago. No—longer than that—12 years ago.

JR: What church do you belong to?

JH: Redeemer Baptist, 24th and went to another church before that—Consolation Baptist Church. Went there about 16 years. So altogether we've been in church about 25 years, 24 or 25 years. I'm a Deacon [and my wife] is a Deaconess.

JR: Did you grow up in a religious family?

JH: They went to church. They wasn't real religious. You know, how your family makes you go to church—that's how it was. Don't get me wrong, now, I did my share of devilment, too, now. Yeah, I did my share of stuff. Gang fighting and that stuff, drinking.

JR: I was going to say, have you

"Anywhere you go, if everybody gets along, you can do just about anything. It keeps the peace down here. You can go to your neighbors to get a cup of sugar, things like that. The white would look out for the black, the black would look out for the white. That's the way it's always been."

Dickinson.

JR: Have you been attending that church your whole life?

JH: How long we been there? [calls to his wife] Selista! How long we been in Redeemer? Oh, 9 years. I ever been in a fight?

JH: I've been through all that, been through all that. When I was a teenager growing up. By 19 that was all over with.

JR: Was your wife [Selista] your

first love?

JH: Oh, no, no, no. I've got children by two other women. I got a son by one woman and two daughters by another. She wasn't my first love.

JR: How old were you two when you married?

JH: Let's see, we only been together about 22 years, but I knew her awhile before we got together. So we been together about 22 years. We've been married, next month it'll be 19 years; 17th of next month.

JR: So what do you like to do when you're not working?

JH: Well, basically I go to church. Run different places with [my wife] and rest. I sing, I'm in the gospel group. We go out and sing at different churches. Basically, that's what I like to do—sing.

JR: Have you been doing that for awhile?

JH: Yeah.

JR: Are you a good singer?

JH: [Laughs] That's what they say. They say I am, I don't know. I don't want to do that, say that I'm good—I don't want to do that. But I do the best I can.

JR: What inspires you to go on?

JH: I got to take care of my baby [his wife]. Just looking at her, I know I got to get out there and go to work. §

"[My family] went to church. They wasn't real religious. You know, how your family makes you go to church—that's how it was. Don't get me wrong, now, I did my share of devilment, too, now."

Selista Hudson, 2002

Mrs. Selista Hudson is a warm and welcoming woman who resides on the 3600 block of Wharton Street with her husband, James Hudson. She has two daughters from her previous marriage. One lives with her, while the other lives nearby. Mrs. Hudson values her relationship with her family. She occupies her time by teaching arts and crafts to senior citizens at her church. Mrs. Hudson cherishes the close connection she feels with her neighbors in the Forgotten Bottom.

"BETWEEN THE TOP AND THE BOTTOM":

AN INTERVIEW WITH SELISTA HUDSON

BY NICOLE FOX

NICOLE FOX: When were you born?

SELISTA HUDSON: March 24th, 1951.

NF: I was told you weren't born here, but in a different neighborhood.

SH: Yes.

NF: Where was that?

SH: South Philadelphia on the 1800 block of South Street.

NF: How long did you live in your original neighborhood before you moved here?

SH: Oh, I was young when I came up here. Well, let's say I was living "up top"—"up top" means 31st and Wharton. And so then I moved down here in 1982. So I've been down here about . . . 22 years. Compared to where I used to live at, most of the people that live "up top" would know one another because most of the people in this area married one another.

NF: [People] who lived up by 31st?

SH: 31st and Wharton, right. Like,

that's how I met my husband because he came up the Top and I came down the Bottom, so we mingled like that.

NF: So where did you first meet your husband?

SH: First I met him down here, but then he was too old for me because back then they called him an "old head"—that means he was older than me.

NF: How much older is he?

SH: He's about eight years older than me, but when I came down here I was like, 14, he was, like, 20. So you knew that wasn't going to work with my mother. But then after we got older we started out as friends and we fell in love with one another. 'Cause I was married before.

NF: So when were you married?

SH: We were married in 1983, but we knew each other for years. But, you know, there were things and we just waited to get married. Plus, I had to get my divorce from my other husband.

NF: So were you married in a church?

SH: Yes, Consolation Baptist Church, 25th and Wharton.

NF: Is that the church you're a part of?

SH: Not right now—I'm part of the Church of Redeemer, 24th and Dickinson.

NF: Why'd you switch?

SH: Because Consolation Baptist Church was becoming a much larger church than I wanted to attend. The Church of the Redeemer is a smaller and more intimate church. I still feel as if I know all of the members.

NF: Do you have any children?

SH: I have two. These two right here [points to pictures of her daughters]. That's the youngest one—she's 30—and the other one—she'll be 32. My oldest one—she acts like me: she's got a lot of mouth. My youngest one, I use her for my strength, like if I have a problem or something like that. The other one I laugh with. It's just, you know, when you have two girls and you're a female, you can bond together. I remember when my children were growing up, he used to hate for the girls to be in the room. He said, "Why all the time they have to be in the room?" I said, they're girls, they want to be with their mom. He said, "Aw, well, I don't like it." You know, he was crazy. I say, that's how you bond together. We're close. He knows that, even now, he says, "Your two daughters—whew." It's nice, though.

Flag flying in the neighborhood, 2002

> "And I have a cousin across the street, my brother's around the corner. Now, my husband—he's related to everybody in the neighborhood. Cousin around the corner, cousin up around there, you know. So it's like when you marry, you marry into the Bottom—that's how I feel."

NF: Do your daughters still live here?

SH: My youngest one does—she's upstairs on the computer.

NF: So do you consider your family to be very close knit?

SH: Oh, we're close. You see, there's four chairs here, four settings here, and that's how it's always been. You know, a household. And I have a cousin across the street, my brother's around the corner. Now, my husband—he's related to everybody in the neighborhood. Cousin around the corner, cousin up around there, you know. So it's like when you marry, you marry into the Bottom—that's how I feel.

NF: Is that how it is for a lot of people?

SH: Around here, that's all you see. They marry the same—their next-door neighbor or around the corner. That's how it is.

NF: Are your daughters from this marriage or the first?

SH: The first marriage. He knows my first husband and they're close too. It's like I said, we all just bind together.

NF: Was your first husband from the same neighborhood?

SH: Same thing—up the street. That's how it was. But it's nice, though, because you know one another, you're raised together, you know their ways and stuff like that. So that's why, I guess, you don't move out of the neighborhood. That's how it is down here: people don't move out of the neighborhood, they just get married and stay here and they grow old.

NF: Are there a lot of people moving into the neighborhood? Like you said, there's a lot of younger people.

SH: A lot of younger people, but they just haven't moved out. They haven't gotten married yet either.

Selista Hudson with neighborhood residents John Olszewski and Elizabeth Rhodes, 2002

You know, back in our age it was like marriage. We believed in marriage. These younger people nowadays, they just live together or don't get married at all. With my daughters, I teach them, "you stay home until you get married."

NF: Is your oldest daughter married?

SH: No, but she just went out on her own, she's still close. They don't have any children—I don't have any grandchildren. They have to get married first. That's what I taught them and they're keeping that, so far. Other than that, everything's all right down here. I like it, you know, did you see how quiet it is when you come in the neighborhood? Even the summertime, it's the same way. After 9 p.m. you don't see anyone on the block, nobody on the streets. It's nice down here.

NF: So everyone pretty much gets along?

"White, Black, Asian—we just get along. I feel when you live in a neighborhood like this you bind together. You know everyone, everyone knows your children—there's a lot of love."

SH: White, Black, Asian—we just get along. No separation around here. I feel when you live in a neighborhood like this you bind together. You know everyone, everyone knows your children—there's a lot of love. You don't want to see your neighborhood go down; you don't want to see anyone come in here and tear your neighborhood down. I don't think I'll ever move out of the neighborhood, unless I move into a smaller apartment. Like, after my youngest daughter leaves maybe I might move into a smaller apartment. But it's going to be hard for me because I like this type of neighborhood—quiet. I like my privacy, I like to come out on my step and just sit there. It's nice down here. Like I said, everyone marries one another, and when their house gets empty, it's like, "well, I'll move next door to mom." That's how it is down here. §

Selista Hudson at a meeting of the Forgotten Bottom Neighborhood Association, 2002

AnnMarie Kerr

AnnMarie Kerr, 2002

A nnMarie Kerr is a single parent who is raising two boys, Brian and Mathew. Born in 1958, she has lived in the Forgotten Bottom all of her life and was raised in the house across the street from the one that she now owns. Two cousins, her aunt and her mother live on the same street as she does. She has worked for a law firm in Center City, Philadelphia for the past 23 years. She believes that the support she has received from her children has been the greatest asset of her life.

"LIFE ISN'T EASY, IT'S NOT A BOWL OF CHERRIES":

AN INTERVIEW WITH ANNMARIE KERR

BY JULIE DUFFIELD

JULIA DUFFIELD: What year were you born?

ANNMARIE KERR: I was born in 1958.

JD: What is your nationality?

AK: My ancestors are from Ireland and Scotland.

JD: Was there pride in your family about your heritage? Like certain traditions?

AK: Not really. My mom came from a very big family of twelve and my dad was a smaller family, but I think they were all born here in America.

JD: So it would be more as if your grandparents were born in a different country?

AK: Yes.

JD: You were born in Grays Ferry?

AK: Yes.

JD: So how was growing up in this neighborhood?

AK: It was great. There were lots of kids in the neighborhood—always had somebody there for you. It was always a great neighborhood in this

section of Grays Ferry per se, as far as people getting along. During the early '70s there were racial problems, but down in this area there has been no problem at all.

JD: Most people that live here call it "the Forgotten Bottom." Is that what you call it?

AK: Actually, it was always called "the Bottom." Forgotten Bottom came when we started to have the neighborhood meetings and the city and other people did not include us in their plans for what they had designed for different areas within the Grays Ferry area.

JD: So it was as if this part of the area was excluded, hence the name "Forgotten Bottom"?

AK: Yes.

JD: When did the group meetings start?

AK: I would say probably about two years ago—in 1999 or 2000.

JD: Is it mostly the people who have been in the neighborhood the longest?

AK: The meetings consist pretty much of the residents who have been here and are still concerned about the neighborhood and what will happen in this neighborhood, if anything. There has not been much change in this neighborhood. It was always considered industrial with businesses in the area, but the newest edition is Fed-Ex. I think the meetings started then because of certain restrictions that the city was going to lay out with regards to street layouts and things like that.

JD: Back to you personally—where was the house that you were raised in?

AK: I currently live on the street where I was raised—my mother is right across the street. The houses on that side of the street are smaller than the ones on this side. They have two bedrooms and these have three, so it was a little tough growing up there with three other siblings and then we had an aunt and an uncle at times who had lived with us. Close-knit, but no privacy. I am the oldest with two sisters

AnnMarie Kerr at the Philadelphia Zoo, 1970

younger than I and the brother is the youngest.

JD: Why did your uncle and your aunt come to live with you?

AK: My aunt lived with us because her parents died at a very young age and my uncle came to live with us after he was in the service.

JD: What did your parents do?

AK: My mom was a stay-at-home mom until my brother was probably in the younger grades and than she worked for Jefferson Hospital in Center City. My father was employed by Philadelphia Gas Works for about 40 years.

JD: What type of values did your parents teach you?

AK: Respect. There was a lot of respect—respect for elders, respect for your neighbors. It was ingrained in me that if I did anything wrong it would go back to my parents. Regardless, mom or dad was going to find out. Always respect for other people, especially elders. In all honesty, again, this neighborhood is pretty diversified. We have had all kinds of people living here and all kinds of people got along. I don't like to say the "n" word but as a kid growing up in the '60s and '70s, that was a big, predominant word used and I don't like it myself and I do not instill that in my kids. I treat people the way I want to be

I remember being jumped by three black girls who were older than I and bigger than I. But somehow I got out of the situation. They grabbed me by the back of my sweater and I scooped out with my arms and I ran. And they stood there holding the sweater. My concern was that I dropped my books. Growing up within that time period, there were lots of problems I would encounter coming home from school because I was pretty much the last white person to get off the bus. I would have to cross into a mixed territory. Once I was

"I remember being jumped by three black girls who were older than I and bigger than I. . . . They grabbed me by the back of my sweater and I scooped out with my arms and I ran. And they stood there holding the sweater."

treated and I think I have learned that from my parents. Regardless of what color you are, you are still a person.

JD: Have you yourself ever dealt with any discrimination against you?

AK: I have. I think I may have been in the fifth or sixth grade, old enough to walk home from school.

in my area, I knew I was fine.

JD: Did you get a diploma?

AK: Yes, I graduated from high school. I held the job that I am still currently with, the same employer, for 23 years. I was married twice and now I'm a single parent.

JD: How old are your kids?

AK: Brian is 22 and Mathew is 13.

JD: When you were younger, how

did you meet boys and girls?

AK: That was the hard part—there weren't really many within. It was always somebody who came into the area from outside the area. Pretty much, always older guys—that was always our threat. I wasn't allowed to leave the house when they were around but it was pretty cool because they would bring their guitars and hang out on the front steps and we would sit there and we would sing songs and hang out right in front of our parents. We couldn't go anywhere to get in trouble—if we got in trouble, we got in trouble right there.

JD: So I guess this would lead to your first love.

AK: Which was someone within Grays Ferry—little bit older than I. At the time I was a little bit rebellious to my parents and pretty much at that point after I graduated from high school I left my parents' residence and went to live with this guy, who I eventually ended up marrying because I was pregnant. I was with him for about two and a half years—he was my first son's father.

JD: And then . . .

AK: My second husband I met on my job. I worked with him. He moved in with me and he helped me with my son and then in '86 we

AnnMarie Kerr at her senior prom, St. Maria Goretti High School for Girls, 1976

were married.

JD: Do you go to church on Sundays?

AK: I do. I consider myself Catholic. I do practice. I am not faithful 100%, but yes, the majority of the time I try to go to church. I have raised my kids Catholic. They have both made all their sacraments to this point. My parents didn't go to church on a regular basis.

JD: So they didn't practice?

AK: They were Catholic but they just didn't go. They made sure that the children went. After I was out of high school that bothered me a lot and I pulled away from the church for awhile but there's always a need for God, however you see it.

> "I couldn't do it without my kids. . . . When I was raising Brian, back in '81 or '82, I paid $150 rent, which was very affordable, and I shoveled coal. . . . You do what you have to, that's what you have to do as a single parent."

That's what pulled me back again.

JD: Is it the same church that you went to as a child that you go to now?

AK: Yes. It's St. Gabriel's. I went to St. Gabriel's School, which is now called Our Lady of Angels School. It started two years ago and it consolidated two other schools, but the parish, the church, is still recognized as St. Gabriel's.

JD: Do you think being a single parent has made you a stronger person?

AK: Oh, it sure has. I couldn't do it without my kids. My kids have gotten me through thick and thin. For an example, when I was raising Brian, back in '81 or '82, I paid $150 rent, which was very affordable, and I shoveled coal. I had coal heat and that's how I kept myself— you do what you have to, that's what you have to do as a single parent. I have always known the owner of the house I live in now and I always admired the way she had

kept her house and ended up buying her house, which is across the street from my parents' house. On this street I have two cousins, one aunt and my mom . . . and a boyfriend.

JD: Now, is your boyfriend the guy who I met when I met you?

AK: Yes. That's Billy. I wasn't one to drink and hang out in bars and most men go to work, come home, kick back, and have a couple drinks before they go home. I didn't realize Billy had his eye out for me for a long time, which I didn't know. We would pass each other and he will tell you today that I used to stick my nose up in the air and walk past him. One day he just walked in and said, "She's here and I want to talk to her." And from there that's how it went and they say, "It's right in your backyard." Well, it's right across the street. It's been a great relationship. We have been together for five years. Mathew was very resentful in the beginning of it but

> **"We would pass each other and he will tell you today that I used to stick my nose up in the air and walk past him. One day he just walked in and said, 'She's here and I want to talk to her.'"**

has come a long way. It's hard for kids.

JD: Do you spend lots of time with your cousins that live on this street?

AK: No, we pretty much all have our own lives. Never was really a close knit family on my mother's side, but we are there for each other when we need each other.

JD: Are you close with your mother?

AK: Yes. My dad passed away a year ago, so it's been a little bit hard not to have him around. Because my siblings don't live in the area and I live right across the street, I'm here. It's hard on me but I've learned to deal with it.

JD: Were you very close with your father?

AK: Yes.

JD: What are some memories that you have of him?

AK: Dad always helped me with school projects. I remember building a castle . . . I was thirteen. And for Christmas, I was into Led Zeppelin and my father gave me a tape of Karen and Richard Carpenter. I thought, "They don't know where I'm at in my life," but I accepted that because that's where they thought I was and in their eyes they didn't want to see me turn a different way and go out of whatever they expected of me.

JD: What do you consider your most treasured possession?

AK: My kids. And being a single mom there are just so many

"And being a single mom there are just so many moments where I can look back and say I'm the one that kisses them goodnight, I get the hugs, I get the grief, and I get the tears."

AnnMarie Kerr with her family

moments where I can look back and say I'm the one that kisses them goodnight, I get the hugs, I get the grief, and I get the tears. I try to treat my kids as individuals who can make their own choices once they reach that age. Until they reach that age, I'm their guiding light. They have to abide by what I say: my house, my rules.

JD: What type of values do you think you have instilled in your children?

AK: Life isn't easy, it's not a bowl of cherries. There are difficulties, but you have to make the best of what you have. Respect people—treat people the way you would want to be treated. I have never seen my children disrespectful to other people. Just accept people for who they are.

JD: What do you think inspires you to go on? What is your guiding

light?

AK: I have to. I don't like being negative. There's always a positive outlook—it could be worse. You never know what's going to happen: you could be up one day and down another. I have lost my hearing. Mathew was two when I lost my hearing and that happened overnight.

JD: What happened?

AK: Through studies they said a blood clot ruptured in my ear and I went completely deaf in one ear and I have a hearing aid. The hearing aid has changed my life. Being a single parent, going through divorce—I made it through all that because of my kids, because of the strength that I have. Only because you have to go on—things could be a lot worse.

JD: Do you feel like the people in the neighborhood are there to support you?

AK: If I want them to be. There are some neighbors who probably wouldn't talk to me and that's fine because they all have their own lives and that's respectable. I can't say I depended on my neighbors to get me through the times that I had to get through. It was more so family and networks at work have gotten me through. There is a bit of a cultural barrier. A lot of the neighbors are Oriental. Years ago it used to be Polish and different nationalities but now it's mostly Orientals. Not knowing their culture, not understanding it, but we all get along. I mean, everyone says hello to everybody, and respects everybody, knows everybody else's business. Sometimes that's good and sometimes that's bad. [Laughs.] I didn't like it when I was dating and I would get home late and someone would know that I was coming in. They know everything, they just know everything. Like I said, it's the same people that yelled at me are yelling at my kids now—it's just that they have lived a long time, you know?

JD: Do you consider yourself to be a lucky person?

AK: Very lucky. Just to enjoy life every day. As a single parent it's hard raising two boys without a positive role model. That saddens me because I think they still need a father figure, which I'm glad that I have a man in my life to provide that because he does.

JD: What about the St. John's club [at 1314 S. 36th, where the Forgotten Bottom Neighborhood Association meets]?

AK: For years it was recognized as St. John of the Jordan and now it's considered AOH Division Seven— it's an Irish club, the Ancient Order of Hibernians.

JD: So how did you become involved in that?

AK: Probably because Billy was involved with that. As a kid I knew it was there, as a club. My mom, in fact, was probably a member because there was a Lady's

"It's those old folks that are here just looking out for each other making sure there's nothing going on. They bring the neighborhood together, keep it together. They are our voice . . . the voice of the Forgotten Bottom."

AnnMarie Kerr, in front of her house, 2002

Membership to St. John of the Jordan Club. The ladies, back then, would hold penny parties and Bingo parties and things like that.

JD: How do you join that type of club? Is everybody in it Irish?

AK: Actually, no. It's pretty much like a "Cheers." It's called the AOH Division Seven but it's just a local place, a neighborhood bar.

JD: Are the neighborhood meetings connected to the club at all?

AK: No, that's just where they hold them. . . . It's those old folks that are here just looking out for each other making sure there's nothing going on. They bring the neighborhood together, keep it together. They are our voice . . . the voice of the Forgotten Bottom.

JD: All in all, what do you think of your neighborhood?

AK: I don't think I'd want to live anywhere else. I really don't. It's quiet, it's quaint. It's so inexpensive to live here. Even for outsiders coming in, I think all people are welcomed. It's just a shame to see the old people die off. It eventually will change 100% once all those people are gone. It's a tight knit community—the people who keep it going are all good people.

JD: What was it like before it changed?

AK: At 30th in Grays Ferry there was a slaughterhouse where the animals were being brought over—I remember that. We would go to the slaughterhouse and see the animals—not being slaughtered but coming off the trucks and I really didn't think anything of it then whereas now I would have a problem with that. Today it would upset me.

JD: You said that animals have been dropped off around here and strays are in the area because of that. And as I understand it, your dog was one of them.

AK: Yes, there are stray animals that have been dumped in this area. She wouldn't take to anybody. There were a lot of neighbors trying to feed her and take her in and what not. Finally, what we did is, there was a little vacant lot that we saw her sleeping in, at night. This was in the dead of winter and she was all curled up and I took the lock off of the gate, left some water, left some food. She kept coming back.

There was one Saturday I was pretty sick. I ended up in the emergency room and Billy took me to the hospital and when I came back home she was in here and she was cleaned and bathed. They had bought her a bowl and bought her a flea collar, and she's one of the best dogs I've ever had.

JD: Do you think a lot of the neighborhood pets were stray animals?

AK: Yes. The older man next door had a stray for years. The woman around the corner had a stray pup.

JD: Who drops them off?

AK: Just people. [petting her dog] She's my girl.

JD: And her name is Girl?

AK: We call her Girl, yeah. I think Mathew came up with that name. She's so good, she's so pretty. §

*Mrs. Helen MacClain talking with students from the Community
Publishing class, 2002*

Mrs. Helen MacClain was born on February 18, 1919, in the Forgotten Bottom, right around the corner from where she lives now. She was born to Dominica and Joseph Olszewski; both parents were immigrants from Poland. Mrs. MacClain was married for 58 years when her husband passed away. She has two children, a boy and a girl. Mrs. MacClain worked her entire life at various jobs, from factories to cafeterias. She is now retired. She enjoys vacationing at the shore and baking her scrumptious cookies.

RYAN MURPHY: When were you born?

HELEN MACCLAIN: I was born February 18, 1919.

RM: Where were you born?

HM: Right around the corner, here in Philadelphia. Right around the corner.

RM: What was the address?

HM: Oh, I don't remember. It was thirteen something. I was born on 36th Street, right off Reed Street.

RM: Who were your parents?

HM: My mother's name was Dominica, and my father's name was Joseph. Their last name was Olszewski.

RM: Where were they from?

HM: Poland. My mother came here when she was 16. I don't know what year my father came. She knew my father in Poland, too, you know, because my father's sister lived across the street, and she married my mother's cousin [laughs].

RM: Can you describe your mother and father?

HM: Well, my father died when I was six years old. He left seven children. The youngest one was six weeks old. My mother kept us all, never got into any trouble or anything. She raised us all. My mother was a hard working person. We were going to public school then. As we got a little bit older, we were Catholic, and we were ready to make our first Holy Communion so

"Well, my father died when I was six years old. He left seven children. The youngest one was six weeks old. My mother kept us all, never got into any trouble or anything. She raised us all. My mother was a hard working person."

123

> "I finished eighth grade, then I went to vocational school. . . . We had it tough. Everything had to be washed, ironed, starched, and you had to dampen the clothes the night before to iron the next day. We had two bushels of clothes a week to be ironed. I can't begin to tell you all the work I had to do."

we went to a Catholic school. We went up to eighth grade in Catholic school and then I went to a vocational school. Some of my sisters went to high school, but my one sister had to quit high school because my mother was getting Mother's Assistance and my sister couldn't be what she wanted to be. They ruled what went on in the household.

RM: Mother's Assistance?

HM: Mother's Assistance—at that time, they were tough. That was a bad time. My sister had to quit high school. The older one, she didn't quit. She went to school one day a week and worked but she wasn't 16 when she quit school. If you were 14, you could go get a job, but you had to go to school one day a week. Things were tough.

RM: What was your educational background?

HM: I finished eighth grade, then I went to vocational school. I took a two-year course in dressmaking, and a postgraduate course for six months. Then that was the end of my education. I had to stay home. My mother was working so I had to take care of the kids and cook the meals from the time I was eleven. My sister left her husband and brought a two-week-old baby and I had to watch him too. We had it tough. Everything had to be washed, ironed, starched, and you had to dampen the clothes the night before to iron the next day. You ironed everything like petticoats and what not because there was no such a thing as slacks in those days. There were only clothes that had to be ironed. We had two bushels of clothes a week to be ironed. I can't begin to tell you all the work I had to do. My two older sisters didn't have to do those things. They were working.

RM: Can you describe Grays Ferry in the time you were growing up?

HM: Oh, it was beautiful. Beautiful around here. This street, Earp Street, we had trees on both sides of the street. We had yellow bricks in the street. It was not asphalt, it was yellow bricks. Thirty Sixth Street, up the street, was big cobbled stones. We had factories all around. This was an industrial area. The homes were always kept very, very nice. We didn't have any houses torn down like we got now. The people that lived here were from the old country, you know. We had Italians, Lithuanians, Slovaks, Polish, Russian, and we had Blacks too. Everybody kept up his or her property. It wasn't like it is today. I mean, I get disgusted when I walk out and see all the trash cans on the street. You never saw that. I never knew how to use a mop. We had to get down on our hands and knees and scrub. We had no heat, all we had was a coal range in the kitchen with a boiler, you know, right there [points to the center of the kitchen] to heat the water. Oh, it was rough. There was no heat through the whole house. In the beginning, we had gaslights. We didn't even have electricity, we had gaslights [laughs].

RM: How did they work?

HM: I can't remember now but I remember a chandelier in the dining room. Upstairs there was a thing that came out of the wall and you turned the gas on and lit it with a match.

RM: That's so different.

HM: Oh, you're not kidding. Things are so different today.

RM: What keeps you living in this

"We had to get down on our hands and knees and scrub. We had no heat, all we had was a coal range in the kitchen with a boiler . . . to heat the water. Oh, it was rough. . . In the beginning, we had gaslights . . . we didn't even have electricity."

Snow Balls
1 cup Butter softened
1 cup 10X sugar
1 cup chopped nuts
1/2 tsp. salt
1 tsp vanilla   Bake 325°
2 cups flour   15 to 18 min.
Cream butter + sugar add salt
+ vanilla beat in nuts +
flour. Shape in 1 inch balls
place on ungreased cookie sheet.
Roll in 10X sugar when the
cookies are baked + still warm.

A recipe from Helen MacClain

neighborhood?

HM: I was born here, raised here. If it weren't that my mother wanted to stay here, we wouldn't have been here today. We were going to buy property in New Jersey, and build a bungalow on top for her. After we put the deposit down, she didn't want to go. So this house was for sale and we bought it. Do you know how much I paid for this house?

RM: How much?

HM: Eighteen hundred dollars. I'd be lucky if I got twenty- five, maybe thirty thousand dollars for it. I'd be lucky, of course, because of location. If it were somewhere else, I could get more. I could get more for my mobile home down the Shore [laughs].

RM: What was the social atmosphere of Grays Ferry like as a teenager?

HM: Well, we had a club around the corner. They used to have a Polish club, which held dances on Saturday night. They had a little Polish band. Then we had things going on at the churches. Things like that. Nothing too much, you know. Not like today.

RM: What type of occupations did you get involved with?

HM: Well, my first job that I ever got, as a child, I took care of children for business people. I lived with them. I done that for awhile and then I got a job in a cigar factory wrapping boxes at Christmas time. After I got married I worked in the mill up on 26th Street working on children's dresses. I was sewing buttons on the children's dresses. I worked at Edward's Shoe Company. During the war I worked at the defense plant—I was a riveter on airplanes. Then I worked in General Electric—I wired switchboards for Russian ships. Then I transferred up to the machine shop. Well, an incident happened and I walked off the job.

RM: What happened?

HM: They put me on this machine that took me half a day to clean. It was filthy—full of dirty oil and shavings. It had five drills on it. The next day this other girl clocked in together with me and she walked over to my machine and I said to her, "That's my machine." She said, "That was your machine." So I called the formative supervisor and I said, "How come she took my machine?" He said, "Well, she has seniority over you." I said, "Thank you," and I walked out. When I went back for my pay, they told me they couldn't use me, to go into another defense plant. That's when I took the job at the Shoe Company.

RM: Was that your last job?

HM: No. Well, I worked at Oscar Meyer, here in Philadelphia when they first came. I was the ninth person hired there. I ran their cafeteria. From there, after they closed the cafeteria down, I didn't want to go into the plant, so I got a job with the school board. I worked in the cafeteria in the schools and then I became a cafeteria manager. That was the last job I had. I retired from the school. I worked through all my married life. I mean, I am still offered jobs, but I won't take them. Oh no. The priest down the Shore, when I am down there, begs me to cook for him on Fridays, the day the cook is off. I say, "I'm retired!" [laughs] I do it when I wanna do it, and if I don't wanna, I don't do it.

RM: When you were employed, what was it like for a woman to get employed?

HM: The jobs weren't too hard to get. There were plenty of jobs around. Pay was low. You didn't make that much money, even during the war. It was high, considering what people used to make. The people I lived with, taking care of their kids, I got $6 a week. I was 16 then—a dollar a day. I would give my mother the $6 because she needed it.

RM: Was there any tension between the male employers and the female employees?

HM: Not really. Not that I know of. I never had any problems.

RM: Was the pay fair?

HM: Oh yes, for that time. Yes, it was good money for the times. Not like they make today. It was good money. That's why I worked, I had

Thumb-print cookies
2/3 cup sugar
1 cup of butter softened
1/2 tsp. almond extract
2 cup all purpose flour
1/2 cup raspberry jam
Heat oven to 356°. In a large
bowl, combine sugar, butter &
almond extract. Beat at medium
speed, scraping bowl often until
creamy. Reduce speed to low, adding
flour. Beat until well mixed
Shape dough into 1 inch balls
Place cookies 2 inches apart on ungreased cookie sheet. With thumb
make indentation in center of each
cookie. Fill each indent with about
a quarter teaspoon of jam. Bake
14 to 18 minutes until edges are
lightly brown. Let stand one minute
Remove from cookie sheet.

A recipe from Helen MacClain.

to help out. My husband used to work at University of Penn. He was only making $18 a week. His grandfather was a trader for the basketball team over there. His grandfather had 25 years of service with the University of Penn. He worked there a long time. Then, when he retired they asked him to give my husband a job there. My husband did not stay there that long because he was going to get drafted, so he came back to the city. He got drafted. He was in service for 19 months and then he got discharged. He got a job in the oil company. Then he got a job at PSFS on Market Street—he was a carpenter for them. I worked from when I was 16 and retired at 62. I had a lot of different jobs. My husband didn't have as many jobs as I had.

RM: Was the work ever endangering to your health?

HM: Not really. No. I didn't think it was. You had to be careful. When I was wiring a switchboard, I had to put two behind and the one I was working with in front. One swung out and hit me in the head. I thought I was sweating. I went like

went to work the next day. I was all right. That's the only time I got hurt while I was working.

RM: Do you feel as a woman you have more rights now than you did growing up?

HM: I don't really know. In some ways, yes. To me, you never thought about rights. I don't know—that's a hard question. I felt if I was to do something, I did it. One thing— growing up, we never knew an older woman by her first name. We had

" . . . I had a very good husband. He thought of his children and his home first. You know, as far as money-wise. He would go out on Saturdays with his friends, drinking, but during the week, nothing. He never missed work for drinking, never."

that [wipes her hand across her forehead] and really I was bleeding [laughs]. That was the only time I ever got hurt, you know, on the job. The defense plant had its own dispensary there—it was like a hospital. They took me down there and fixed me up and told me that if I got a headache in the middle of the night to come right back there. They were afraid of a concussion. I

to call her "Mrs. So and So," whatever her last name was. I never found out the older women's names until I got married. When we were children, we never, ever heard anybody say, "Annie" to a grown up. It was "Mrs. So and So." We were taught a lot of respect for our elders. That was one thing I can say that the kids today don't have. There's a difference with the kids being brought up today and the way we were raised. My children had to call a person by "Mrs. So and So." They weren't allowed to say their first name—no way. Thank God I had two good kids. A lot of neighbors would tell me they were good kids.

RM: How long were you married?

HM: I was married for 58 years when my husband passed away. That was six years ago. I was married a long time. People thought it wouldn't last because we ran away and got married [laughs]. They didn't even know I got married until I was pregnant [laughs]. Then I went to live with my mother-in-law—sorriest day of my life. That's where I learned to mop a floor. My mother never had a mop. We didn't have rugs. We had linoleum that looked like a rug. They were printed. We had to get down on our hands and knees and scrub throughout the entire house, then the yard and the alley too. We had to clean. Oh yeah, every week.

RM: How many children do you have?

HM: Two. A boy and a girl.

RM: What was it like to be employed and raise your children?

HM: My mother lived next door. She didn't go to work until after I came home from work, so it wasn't too bad for me. I had somebody to look after the kids until I got home. It was rough because I had to do everything at night, when I came home. On Saturdays was when I got done all my cleaning. During the week I would have to wash clothes and iron and stuff like that. I made sure they got their homework done and cooked their meals. When they got a little bigger they were allowed to stay home by themselves. My daughter used to have a lot of her friends come over when she was in high school. They used to come here after school, play music and dance because I allowed it. My mother didn't know that I knew about it. I used to meet the kids going to the trolley car—at that time we didn't have buses, we had trolley cars. They were all going home when I was coming home from work. My mother had mentioned to me one day and I said, "Yes, mom, I know she has kids coming. I told her she could do it. I know where she's at." My mother said, "okay," and said nothing about it. She thought my daughter was making them leave before I came home from work. See, that's where she got the impression that I didn't know. When I came in here, there wasn't a thing out of place. I know those kids were good kids. When she was having her sixteenth birthday party we were remodeling then. I told her, "You kids can do whatever yous want." They rolled up all the rugs, they danced, and they had their party. Then they came back the next day and cleaned everything up; they cleaned and finished everything they didn't finish the day before. They were nice kids. I couldn't complain about them—really nice kids.

RM: And finally, would you consider yourself to be a strong, independent woman?

HM: Yes [laughs]. I guess you can see that. I handled all the finances. My husband didn't want to handle any money. He would come home from work, take so much out of his pay for spend money and give me the rest. If he needed something, he got it. I paid all the bills, bought the kids all of their clothes, went shopping. I handled the finances, not because I wanted to, but my husband didn't want to do it. He said, "If I saw something that I wanted, I wouldn't think about a bill that had to be paid. I would just go buy it." That's why he didn't want to handle the money. He really couldn't do it. One time, when the bank statements came in, I used to open and look at it and go out and check it to make sure my balance was the same as the bank. He said to me, "What are you hiding?" This was after the children moved out. I said, "What do you mean? I'm not hiding nothing." He said, "Well, whenever it comes, you take it and go out there and put it away." I said, "Well, I figured you don't want to be bothered with it." So, the next Saturday, I handed it to him, and he opened it and said, "I don't know what it's all about" [laughs]. I said, "Don't ever accuse me of hiding anything. I don't have to hide anything." He knew where the money was—if he needed something he took it, but he always told me what he took, always. I mean, I had a very good husband. He thought of his children and his home first. You know, as far as money-wise. He would go out on Saturdays with his friends, drinking, but during the week, nothing. He never missed work for drinking, never. §

John Olszewski on his front porch, 2002

B orn to recent Polish immigrants in 1914, John Olszewski has lived his entire life in the Forgotten Bottom. His father died in 1925 and his mother raised seven children on the same street where Mr. Olszewski lives now. His sister, Helen MacClain, also a life-long neighborhood resident, lives just up the street from her brother. Mr. Olszewski is the father of two children, a daughter, and a son who fought and died in the Vietnam War at the age of 18. He has held numerous jobs during his working days, from Westinghouse to Sylvan Seal Dairy to Pennwalt, where he worked as a machinist for 23 years. Mr. Olszewski is now retired and lives with his second wife, to whom he has been married for 31 years.

JOHN OLSZEWSKI: You asked— was I was born in this neighborhood and when?

STEFANIE WOOLRIDGE: Uh huh.

JO: Oh, 11-17-16. Couple years ago.

SW: A few! [laughs] What year was your house built?

JO: A few. [laughs] Yeah. What year was my house built? I'd say the house, I think it was built about 1914.

SW: You were born in this neighborhood—

JO: Yeah—

SW: Where?

JO: A midwife was the one that took care of everything.

SW: Oh.

JO: See, my mother was a foreigner born in Poland and she came over here when she was 15. And her aunt was supposed to meet her and her aunt got the dates mixed up and she was sitting on Ellis Island there not knowing what happened, nobody to meet her.

SW: Oh!

JO: And she can't speak a word of

"My mother was a foreigner born in Poland and she came over here when she was 15. And her aunt was supposed to meet her and her aunt got the dates mixed up and she was sitting on Ellis Island there not knowing what happened, nobody to meet her. . . . And she can't speak a word of English—"

133

Graphic from the Central High Yearbook 1933

English—

SW: Right—

JO: So some man befriended her and luckily he took her to the end. That's how she got here. Otherwise, I guess she would have had to stay there all day and night, you know. Well, then she moved into what they called Kulmont.

SW: Kulmont?

JO: PA. It's a small mining town. And that's where she met my father. I guess they got married there. I'm not sure about that, but I think they must have got married there. And then they had seven children. And my father died in this house. No, not this house—3609, up the street. He had—he was diabetic. They didn't know what it was. And

he died in 1925, 38 years old.

SW: That's a shame.

JO: Yeah, left my mother with seven children.

SW: And what did she do?

JO: She kept us all together. She worked and kept us together and one by one we helped her out as we went to work. I myself gave her my pay until a week before I got married. I was married twice, but the first time. And I bought this house here. Uh, I forgot. Well, I . . . No, wait a minute, I just—well. It was over 50 years ago. And it was a wreck. I put everything together. I just about rebuilt everything in here. If you had an electric thing or anything that was a hole in the wall, I became a pretty good plasterer and everything else [laughs] Put a new back on the . . . on electric work and everything else. So that's how the house got together.

SW: What number child were you? In the seven?

JO: Well, let me see. I was the third. I had two older sisters. Then I came, and then that woman was here . . . [Helen MacClain, his sister, who lives up the street] she was next. And then I had a brother after her, and three, two sisters after him.

SW: And they've all dispersed?

JO: Yeah.

SW: Except your sister?

JO: One lives in Virginia. One lives over in Jersey. She [Mrs. MacClain] lives up at 11, up the street here. And I live at 23 with my wife.

SW: What did your parents do? Like, what did your mom do?

JO: Well, actually, she was a cleaning woman in the Atlantic building. That was on Broad Street. Atlantic Refining had a big office building on Broad Street. And she worked there. I think it was Broad and Pine, if I'm not mistaken, or somewhere near there.

SW: When you grew up here, what did you guys do for fun?

JO: What's this?

SW: What did you do for fun? I remember you told me you used to swim in the Schuylkill.

JO: Yeah, well, we swam in the Schuylkill. It was pretty dirty water. [laughs] But we used to go over to Kingsessing Recreation Center. It was quite a distance to go to and you were allowed an hour swimming. And—

SW: In a pool.

JO: Pool, yeah. City pool.

SW: Did you have to pay?

JO: No, it was a city pool.

SW: But you only were allowed one hour?

JO: One hour. And what—you'd try to dry your clothes up, your trunks up, before to get in again. If they were damp they wouldn't let you in, you know.

SW: And did they have separate girl swims and boy swims or—

JO: Girls day and boys day. They alternated.

SW: What games did you play?

JO: Well, mostly we picked up games of any sort, you know. Baseball or something like that.

SW: Were toys a big thing?

JO: Oh, well, you more or less picked anything for a toy.

SW: And it was fun!

JO: Yeah [laughs]. Yeah, like, here, at that time, sometimes the streets were iced up, you know. You went out and chopped the ice. Break it

---

"The first thing I remember, see, my mother was getting assistance from the city, I guess, and you had to let [Mothers' Assistance] know—like, we got a Victrola. And we had to say my cousin bought it for us and he had to verify it."

Caption for John Olszewski's yearbook photo, Central High School 1933

up and everything else. You'd have a hatchet or an ax and broke up the street. And use that for recreation.

SW: You just chopped up the ice? And that was fun?

JO: Yeah, well. More or less, you know, at that time.

SW: That'd be like work now, like—

JO: Yeah, well, we don't have the winters we had then. We had some pretty good winters. Sometimes the streets were packed with six inches of ice and all, so you chopped it away to clear the street up.

SW: And did your family have a car? A TV? Radio?

JO: Well, there was nothing like a TV at the time, at my younger age. The first thing I remember, see, my mother was getting assistance from the city, I guess, and you had to let them know—like, we got a Victrola. You had to wind it, you know.

SW: When was that? Do you remember?

JO: Oh my God, no.

SW: A long time ago!

JO: A long time ago! When there was nothing like electric, you know. You wound it with a hand wind job.

SW: Right.

JO: So we got one. Well, it was something like that [points to a brown, stand-up case in the corner of the room, near the TV] in a case and all. And we had to say my cousin bought it for us and he had to verify it. Because you weren't allowed to get things like that unless, you know—

SW: It was a gift.

JO: Yeah. At that time.

SW: Well, what did you do during vacation times? Did you go to the beach or—

JO: Well, I remember, somebody'd take us and, like, Riverview Beach—you ever heard of it? Riverview Beach. You go by boat, you go on the Delaware by boat.

SW: In New Jersey?

JO: No. I don't know. I think it might have been in New Jersey, you know. I'm not sure because it was quite awhile ago. Yeah, that would

> "And the tutor asked me—he called my name out and asked me to stand up. 'Now here,' he said, 'You know you got the highest mark anybody ever got in this test?'"

be a day outing, but there was no such thing as like a week vacation or such.

SW: Oh, no?

JO: No. Well, my sister— The only time I remember being away for about a week was down at North Wildwood. Spent a week there with my sister and her husband. Like, I'm very pale, and one time I fell asleep, and I got burned so bad I could never stay in the sun after that. It blistered up and everything else.

SW: For school, did all your brothers and sisters go to school?

JO: Well, yeah, we all went to school. Like, I remember my mother taking me up to the school, left me on the corner and said, "Go ahead. This is it. I've started first grade." Well, I stayed there, I think, to the fifth grade and then I went to a parochial school. And they put me back one grade. And I kept after the nuns. I said, "I don't belong . . . I belong in a higher grade." After a month I was put in a higher grade. And at the end of the year, I

skipped a grade. They put me in fourth and I argued I had to be in the fifth, and at the end of the year I skipped to the seventh.

SW: Really!

JO: Yeah. And when I went to the eighth grade, we were transferred over to another school, another parochial school, because we were in another boundary. And we had to go to 5th and—I was going to Third and Fitzwater to a parochial school there, St. Stanislaus. And then I was transferred over to St. Mary's over on 59th and Elmwood because we were in another boundary and I was the first graduate there, at that school.

SW: First graduate?

JO: Yeah, the first graduate. We had six girls and three boys in our eighth grade.

SW: That's it!?

JO: Yeah. Six girls, three boys. And then I went to Central High School. And I graduated from there.

SW: What year did you graduate?

JO: 1933.

SW: And then college wasn't—

JO: No, well I, I went to Swarthmore two days.

SW: Yeah?

JO: Well, what happened—I was working in a dairy and then I took an apprenticeship— Well, I had to take a test, an aptitude test for an apprenticeship for a machinist at Westinghouse. And the tutor asked me—he called my name out and asked me to stand up. "Now here," he said, "You know you got the highest mark anybody ever got in this test?" And I knew the answer to the question—one question I left out and I knew the answer to that and I told him that, too. So Westinghouse paid me to go to Swarthmore. And I went two days. My first wife, she started yelping, "You're never home. You're never home. Going to school. Going to work. You're never home." And I, like a fool, quit. So that was my college education. But I did work up to a toolmaker in a jet lab at Westinghouse. I worked there for 12 years and we lost our contract and I had to go look for work somewhere else. So I went over to Campbell Soup and took a job there as a maintenance machinist. And I—

SW: When was that?

JO: Well, 12 years later. Well, I graduated in '33. Seven would be '40. And 12 years there— '52. But the company wanted me to stay there—keep my job because I could machine parts as well as install them. But the union didn't want one—they wanted to teach their men, the maintenance men, how to be machinists. Well, I figured, I wasn't going to get in this argument, so I quit and went to the job I retired from. I went to Pennwalt Company as a machinist. And I

Photo of John Olszewski from Central High School 1933

138

> **"And the three of us got a job as pumper's helpers. . . And I was the only Polish one. The other . . . three [were] Irish. And the boss was Irish. . . . So he called my name out and said, 'You go back to the office. I don't need you.'"**

stayed there until I retired in 1941, because I remembered—no, not 1941. Well, I retired 23 years ago.

SW: So, that would be like—

JO: '87, I think it was. It'd come out to '87. And I went to Pennwalt 23 years before that. I worked there for 23 years. And that was it. That was my career [laughs].

SW: What was—during that time, what was the pay for—

JO: Well, I'd say about $35 a week or so.

SW: As far as working conditions— I mean, you can just speak from your own experience—but how many hours a week did you work?

JO: Me? Well, sometimes I worked— I'd take overtime any time they had it [laughs]. I used to work—a good while there I'd work a second shift. And they'd ask me to work half a shift. I'd only get time and a half with half a shift and for the rest of the shift I'd get double time. So I used to tell them, "I can't do it because there's no trolley run-

ning." I had a car, but I told them I had to wait for a trolley and I couldn't do it. So I'd have to work a double shift or nothing, and I'd get out at seven in the morning. So a lot of times I'd work from 3 o'clock to seven in the morning.

SW: And was that typical, or that was just—

JO: Every once in awhile. I mean, quite often, and that was at Westinghouse. But normally I worked a 40-hour shift.

SW: Did women work there?

JO: Not in that type of work. Women weren't involved in most of that, you know. It was mostly men—

SW: And then, was there racial dynamics in the companies or—

JO: I guess at the time there was. Years and years ago, you know. Well, for example, one time I figured the plant was going to close when I worked at Westinghouse. So I went over to Atlantic Refining for a job and two fellas—the other two fellas were with me. They rode— I had a car and they didn't, so they rode to Atlantic with me. And we got there—the three of us got a job as pumper's helpers. And we were supposed to go together into the— We went to the foreman and somehow or other a fourth fellow was sent. And I was the only Polish one. The other one, or three, Irish. And the boss was Irish. Now this is sent there back. He said, "Well, I don't want you." I was Polish and the other three were Irish and he was apparently Irish. So I stayed there two days and I got a lousy job there. I went back to Westinghouse. Forgot about Atlantic Refining [laughs]. But essentially I went there because I was working as a machinist, but at that time you had to go start over and learn their sys-

> "My foreman wouldn't give me a raise and I went parading in front of the supervisor's window and he called me in. . . . I told him I turned out more work than anybody ever did. . . . He said, 'Well, how much you want?' and I said, '$2.'"

racial, too, in a way. So he called my name out and said, "You go back to the office. I don't need you." And I said, "Well, they wanted the three of us together." He said, "I don't want you. Go back to the office and tell them." So I went back to the office and the guy that was hiring me, he told me to go back and tell him that he wants me to stay with the other two fellas and to send the fourth fella that was tem and all before you could take a machinist job at Atlantic Refining. They had to teach you and everything—you take an apprenticeship there. But I stayed there a couple of days and walked out. Went back to Westinghouse and I stayed there until I— By a week or two, I got laid off because I was hired at that time. And that's when I went to Campbell Soup. I worked there— I don't know how many months, six or eight or so. And, like I told you, I got in a squabble with the union of the company and I figured I— I went to Pennwalt there and stayed there for the rest of my working days.

SW: There seems like there was a lot of work.

JO: There was plenty of work.

SW: Not like today.

JO: No, no. Well, my first job—I got out of high school and I wasn't old enough to work. At that time you had to be 18 and have working papers to show you were 18. Well, I was only 17 when I graduated. I was 16 when I started my senior year and graduated 17. I had to take a lousy job where it only paid $12 a week at that time. And I even went on strike myself because I was putting out more work than any-body ever did before in that particular job. My foreman wouldn't give me a raise and I went parading in front of the supervisor's window [laughs] and he called me in. He said, "What's your problem?" I told him I turned out more work than anybody ever did and I ought—I want— He said, "Well, how much you want?" and I said, "$2." Well, he said, "Suppose we split it and take a dollar more a week?" So I was making $13 [laughs]. I was there two different years. And then that's when I got a job in Sylvan Seal Dairy and I stayed there for over 7 years. But I was making $40 and another fella that was doing comparable work, he was only mak-ing $30.

SW: Why?

JO: Well, I did better work. I was

four years of universal depression have elapsed since the memorable day in September, 1930, when first we felt the glow of knowledge on our green and tender minds. These four years, however, have been glorious ones for us. Through the medium of dear old Central we have acquired knowledge, made friends, and built our characters. Since these three things are the attributes of a polished man, we are, with modesty and hope, ready now for the larger field of Life.

The road before us lies uncharted; we are eager to step out upon it. But before we go, let us be reassured by a backward glance at our life in school. In the pages of this record, we shall read the reminiscences of one of the most promising classes that has ever gone out into the world from the shelter of old Central.

From the Introduction to the Central High Yearbook: text from a salutation to the members of the graduating class of 1933

141

able to do more than him and all. He was always running and he made mistakes and all that, so they didn't pay him as much.

SW: So there wasn't— They could sort of arbitrarily decide what you were paid depending—?

JO: Well, yeah. There was no union or anything, so being that I was able to do more than he was—that I did more work—different types of work in the dairy that he didn't do, I got more money. But then he found out I was making $40, so they gave him a couple of dollars raise, and I had to go at that. I worked there over 7 years and that's when I went to Westinghouse.

SW: What about Barrett?

JO: Well, I lived in the neighborhood and Barrett's was here. I knew quite a few people. And Barrett's originally started—they had a plant from Reed St. around to Wharton and up to 36th and then up to Grays Ferry. And they filled all that in. And they used to get their paper in big—felt paper—in big rolls on boxcars. They came in—they had railroad cars come in and bring the paper. And for years and years that's the way they existed. Then Barrett's was bought by Celetex and Celetex built out to the railroad further and they made their own paper. So there were no more trains coming down

with the paper and all, so they didn't need tracks anymore. And they eventually closed up and just let the place go to the devil.

SW: When did they close?

JO: Oh, I couldn't tell you that. A good while ago. They made shingles, like roofing paper shingles, stuff like that. And rolls of tar paper for roofs and what not. And then it became a vacant property and just went to the devil. Celetex closed the plant and left.

SW: And what did that do to the— I mean, did a lot of people in the community work there at that time?

JO: Yes, quite a few people. Well, practically the whole neighborhood worked in different plants that were around the neighborhood here. We were more or less at that time surrounded by different plants. There was Oscar Meyer's—remember Oscar Meyer's?

SW: Oh yeah.

JO: Well, you still see it. At first it was Vogt's and then Oscar Meyer took it over. Consolidated Dressed Beef was on Grays Ferry, the stockyards were there on Grays Ferry, and Dupont's was along there. Quite a few of the neighborhood people worked in Dupont's. And then there was a leather works here. They were warehousing and then they made containers and things like that they bought and sold. And then there was a rubber works along Schuylkill Avenue where Barrett's—before—up to Barrett's. And then Barrett's from Reed Street on. And then there was a plant that repaired motors—they renovated motors. They were down on Schuylkill Avenue, right by the railroad beyond Reed Street. And people had work. The neighborhood had work all over, you know. And quite a few of them worked on the railroad too.

SW: Was Barrett's one of the last to leave? I mean, slowly it seems like the companies all sort of left.

JO: Yeah.

SW: And was Barrett towards the end of that—?

JO: Well, everybody else got jobs somewhere else, I guess.

SW: But, I mean, was Barrett's or Celetex—were they one of the last companies to leave the area?

JO: Leave there, yes. Dupont's was originally just making paint. Now they're—Well, they still experiment with different paints and all. They experiment— They have scientists there, and all that, to experiment with different things for Dupont. And they're on Grays Ferry and they're still here, you know. And there's some— Well, there's not as many people work on the railroad

as they used to, but there's people that are occupied on the railroad, too, from the neighborhood.

SW: Now.

JO: Yeah.

SW: When did the companies leave?

JO: Well, actually the company that was on Reed Street that took over where the leather works was—they had a seven-alarm fire. That's a bad fire. And that was the end of that company. Barrett's, they left—I guess it might have been 20 years ago.

SW: So, like in the '80s.

JO: Yeah, in the '80s. And the rubber works—I don't remember much about it because that property was taken over by Shell Refining. They had tanks down there and stuff and they stored oil and all that down where the rubber works was, so the rubber works left. So, little by little, just about all the industry left the neighborhood.

SW: Well, I mean, the '80s makes sense because that's sort of when the economy made that shift into the service—

JO: Right. I would say, one of the last ones to leave was Zuckerman, the container place that had the seven-alarm fire. Well, then, where they repair the motors—was called Electric Apparatus—they left after that. They left about ten years ago.

John Olszewski, among the first graduates of St. Mary's of Czestochowa Primary School 1929

And somebody else is still using the building. He's making up shelving and stuff like that out of metal parts. And they maybe have one office girl and two or three people working in the building. That's about it. They—

SW: It's all machines and—

JO: Yeah, well, they cut up, assemble, and all, and make shelves. Metal shelves for storage.

SW: Well, where do people work in the neighborhood now? You said the railroads. And I guess, does anybody work at the FedEx—?

JO: FedEx now? From the neighborhood, there's nobody working there. They had promised people jobs here, but I guess nobody actually—The way I see it, they had to put in an early application. I don't think anybody ever put it in. Now they're yelling. Well, we're having a meeting tomorrow, and that's one of the things they'll be bringing up—about FedEx not hiring nobody from the neighborhood. But they wanted a high school graduate, or equivalent, and be able to handle—well, if you're worked in the plant itself, to handle 75 pounds unassisted.

SW: Oh my goodness!

JO: I can't lift 20 pounds now! [laughs] I have a hard time picking up the coffeepot, anymore. As you get older, you get weaker. And that's one requirement, so—

SW: And they didn't tell anybody that.

JO: Well, they did. They put folders on windshields and all in the neighborhood. And a lot of people never got it. I took one off a windshield so I knew what they were asking for and all, and I told people what they wanted and all. So now the people are saying they didn't hire nobody. They promised jobs. Well, if nobody applied and nobody was fit to do what they want, they didn't hire them, you know.

SW: So where do the people in the neighborhood work?

JO: That I couldn't tell you. Oh, well, they're scattered. Like my wife, she works for K-Mart. She's younger than I am and she works at K-Mart. She's been there over 20 years. She used to do hair dressing, but the stink got to her and all. You can't stay with that too long, you know. Permanents and stuff like that—it's too much for you.

SW: Were you ever in the service?

JO: Oh, I was never in the service. I was called up three times but I never made it. I guess I was in war work in Pearl Harbor. Well, after Pearl Harbor I went to work. Something was being produced for the war effort. Well, I went to Westinghouse and the first job I had there was in the marine division. We're making turbines for ships. You know what a turbine is?

SW: Yeah, the—

JO: Yeah, the propulsion instrument. And then I went to the jet division. I think actually we made the first Navy jet engine. At that time. Then I got promoted to a toolmaker job in the jet lab and we—experimental lab—and we experimented with different things for the jet engines and all.

SW: Did any of your brothers or sisters go in the service?

JO: Yeah, my brother went into the Navy, but none of the sisters. 'Course they weren't called at that time. So my brother went into the Navy during the war.

SW: Which one?

JO: Second World War. He was a gunner on a merchant ship. That was a lousy job, you know. Because a lot of merchant ships were shot out of the water. Submarine come up and hit them and all that. But he survived. He retired at 65 and he died. He had cancer of the intestines. Then died—didn't last long.

SW: How about when Kennedy was shot?

JO: When Kennedy was shot . . . . I really don't—didn't pay much attention to those things.

SW: No?

JO: No. I mean, I knew about it and everything else, but I wasn't one to get excited too much about it. I mean, it's just one of them things that happened.

SW: So Martin Luther King or Malcolm X—you had no strong emotions towards these.

JO: Well, actually, I wasn't too racially orientated. I mean, more or less I accepted people as they were all the time. So it was no big problem as far—sometimes I figure Martin Luther King went too far or something like that, you know. And to me, I . . . I never was too prejudiced or anything like that. So it didn't sink in too much and it didn't matter too much to me. I mean, they yelled and sometimes I yelled, I figured they were yelling about too much, you know. As time went along, they got there ins and all and are doing pretty good. I think as far as the Black race now, they're doing better then we are, you know. Getting things done for themselves and all because they go out after it. And I don't regret—I don't mind them getting it because they go get it. Where we just lay back, more or less, and don't worry about it. So

that's it as far as that's concerned but we're— In the neighborhood, the Blacks and whites get along very well. In this neighborhood, you know. We have our meetings, everybody gets along pretty good.

SW: How about the Vietnam War?

JO: Well, I had a son. He went in as a Paratrooper when he was 17 during the Vietnam War.

SW: Was he drafted or did he—?

JO: No, he volunteered. He said, "Dad, I want to go in." So—well, at that time I was separated and I had the boy. I had two children originally, but then I took my first wife to court and they awarded the girl to the wife and let me have the boy. Well, they asked the kid, "Who do you want to go with?" So the boy said he wants to go with dad and the girl said, "I want to go with mom." And that judge agreed. I contested it, but he said, "That's where the kids want to go." But he went in the Paratroopers in the 82nd Airborne when he was 17. Then he got $5,000 to volunteer to go to Vietnam to replace somebody in the 101 Paratroopers. And he got killed. He didn't last very long. He was just 18 and he was killed—friendly fire. You know what that is, don't you? Friendly fire—our shell fell short and it killed him. You know. And that was the end of my son. He was just 18 years old. I buried him here at St. Peter and Paul cemetery—that's in Springfield. Yeah. And all. That was him. He got the Purple Heart for that. That's about all.

SW: And what was your son's name?

JO: Johnny. John.

SW: That's your name, right?

JO: Yeah. My name's John, too. Yeah.

SW: Oh, OK . On to a lighter subject.

JO: Yeah, what's this?

SW: I said, on to a lighter subject.

JO: Oh, all right. Go ahead.

SW: When you were younger, how did boys meet girls? Like, did you date, or did you—?

JO: Yeah, well you more or less— you dated, you know, but most of the time—well, at first, most of the time I met girls from the neighborhood, you know. And later on— Well, like my first wife—I met her through . . . my cousin was going with her before me. And I was attracted to her. And I approached her and all. She lived in Darby and she was working where I used to go at lunch sometimes. And I got to know her and all. And then—yeah, through that we got married. That's the way we met.

SW: How long did people normally date?

JO: Ah, it was no different than it is now—

SW: Just random—

JO: No, maybe—I didn't date too long. I'd say, maybe six months or so.

SW: That's so fast [laughs].

JO: Yeah. Well, like the first, second wife—I don't know—I'd have met—I'd say—I took her out for awhile. She had two kids. I raised them, too. And we didn't date that long before she wanted to get married. So I said, "Well, I'm too old." I told her, "I'm too old for you," you know. She said, "Well, let me be the judge."

SW: How old were you then?

JO: Uh, 52.

SW: And how old was she?

JO: Uh, 30, I think. I was almost 25 years older than my wife. Present wife. And we're married— it'll be 31 years this June.

SW: That's great.

JO: Yeah, we stayed together. But she more or less accepted— The reason my first wife and I got— She gave me five years to live in this home in this neighborhood and then get out. So I told her to get out.

SW: You didn't want to leave.

JO: No, I didn't want to leave. I mean, I put so much money and time in the house. I worked here. I worked in the house for six months. Went from here, took a bath and went to work every day. Fixed the house up and all. And put my dear time in and all, so she wasn't satisfied. Well, actually, she was— She wanted to leave and so I told her to leave and that was it.

SW: And how long were you married before? The first time?

JO: Twelve years. I moved many times. And we moved into a new home, but we couldn't buy it at that time because it was essentially for war workers at the time. And I figured I was going to buy another house. And that's when I came here.

SW: Back home.

JO: Back home. Yeah, more or less. I lived— My mother lived at 9 and I bought this place and remodeled it. I got it—believe it or not, I bought it for $1300. One thousand three hundred dollars [laughs].

SW: Just imagine.

JO: Because it was a shell.

SW: Have you ever been in a fight?

JO: Yeah. Fight. Yeah. First fight I was in, I quit. Guy hit me in the ear. It was a cold day and, boy, did it hurt! I quit.

SW: How old were you?

JO: Well, then I was about 14 or so.

SW: Why were you in a fight?

JO: That I don't know [laughs]. My cousin, he was instrumental in having me get in a fight with this other kid. Then I had a fight— I was going down the street with a wagon, and a fella—he was learning to be a boxer on the next street—he knocked me off the wagon. I had a fight with him and, well, he finished up, he was laying on the ground. And all his friends jumped me because they didn't like the idea of him losing. They figured he was going to beat me up bad. And then another time I had a fight around the corner with a fella. He turned out to be my best friend. And he said I had a rock or something in my hand. I hit him, I put a lump on his head. And I said, "Look, I have nothing in my hands. Let's go at it again." And he said, "Never mind." So that was it. I don't remember anymore. I mean, I wasn't much of one to get into fights, you know.

SW: That's more fights than I've ever heard of in my life [laughs].

JO: Oh, it was easy to get into fights here. When I went to Central I had one big white fellow on one side and a big Black fella on the other side. Well, I was able to help them, you know, on their lessons and all that. And nobody bothered me there. But that was easy. As far as fellas were concerned, it was easy

to get in a fight. Right. You would-
n't understand that, but me . . . .

SW: What is your most treasured
possession?

JO: What's this?

SW: What's your most treasured
possession?

JO: Possession? I don't know. Well,
I guess my car.

SW: Your car?

JO: Yeah.

SW: How long have you had it?

JO: Oh, this one here I bought
brand new in '99. But when I
worked in Warminster I used to get
a car every two years because I had
a lot of traveling—25 miles each
way. That's 50 miles at least every
day.

SW: So what do you do all day?

JO: What do I do? Now? Oh . . .

SW: Bum around [laughs].

JO: [Laughs] Bum around. More or
less. Well, like, I get up in the
morning. I get everything—Well, I
feed the cat. Put something out for
the dog, set the table up. I pour the
orange juice or whatever I have to
do. It all depends. Make the coffee.
[laughs] know. And then sometimes— Like yesterday, we had half
a dozen shirts to iron. I ironed
them [laughs]. Well, she's working,
you know. So I ironed— A lot of
times I wash the wash and stuff like
that. So the day goes by.

SW: There's always something to
do.

JO: Always something to do. Yeah.
And then usually by 4:00 I watch
the news. And that goes into—
Well, today she's working to 7:00,
you know. And sometimes she
works until 11:00, so I go to bed. I
don't stay up until 11:00. I used to
stay up, but nowadays I— After I
had the heart work done, the stints
put in. And then I've got numerous
pills to take. They keep me alive
[laughs]. After I take the pills I'm
sick for awhile, you know, you
get— They sort of make you dizzy
and everything else. The pills. So
my wife don't realize it, but it's a
good while before I become myself
again. Like, after you take them
you're in dreamland, more or less

SW: You still look great.

JO: Yeah, well. The average person,
85 years old, isn't as versed as I am.
You know, more or less. I mean, I'm
bragging now, but, still, it's true.
People don't believe it, you know,
when I tell them. Like, at the meetings and all, I always got my mouth
open for something or other.

SW: You're very active.

JO: Yeah. Well, I used to do a lot of
things for the neighborhood, too.
Get things done and all—through
the political end. Like, work with
councilmen and stuff like that for

different things. Like, we needed lights on the street. I went around with a petition and everything else and got lights put on the street. And I had the streets paved down here by poking into this and that. And did a lot for the neighborhood. You never get credit for it, you know, but it's just one of those things. §

Lillian Ray and her brother Arthur Gaines, 2002 (Mrs. Ray is holding a photograph of her family members taken in the 1940s)

A lifetime resident of Philadelphia, Lillian Ray has been married for 44 years and is the mother of seven sons and two daughters. In 1988 Lillian was appointed the Deputy Assistant to the Office of Drug Control Policy for the City of Philadelphia. She currently serves in that capacity. The primary mission of the Mayor's Office for Drug Control Policy is to coordinate a multifaceted approach to eradicating drugs and crime in Philadelphia's neighborhoods. Mrs. Ray's work has inspired many communities to organize and speak out against the impact of drugs. Her current project is the formulation of "Grays Ferry Unified," a multi-ethnic organization comprised of religious, social, civic and residential members. The group's mission is to promote and maintain peace and unity throughout the Grays Ferry area. Mrs. Ray is founding a new business in the Forgotten Bottom neighborhood—a restaurant called Melee's will be opening in June 2002.

"A UNIFIED EFFORT":

AN INTERVIEW WITH LILLIAN RAY

BY SUSANNA STEWART

SUSANNA STEWART: Where were you born?

LILLIAN RAY: I was born in Philadelphia, Pennsylvania on Grove Street in the 1300 block in Grays Ferry.

SS: What is your national ancestry?

LR: My maternal parent is from Virginia and my father is from New Jersey.

SS: Where were you raised?

LR: I was raised on Grove Street in Grays Ferry.

SS: Do you have any children?

LR: Yes, I have nine children—I have seven sons and two girls.

SS: Where were they raised—in the same neighborhood as you?

LR: Yes they were.

SS: Would you say that your neighborhood contributed to the way you were raised?

LR: Yes. It was very much contributing to the way that I was raised because we were more or less a large unified family. Everyone was close enough to know about each other's so-called business and we

could also be chastened by numerous people because of them knowing each other. So it played a large part in making us a unified family.

SS: Can you describe your childhood? For example, the events that stand out in your memory growing up in the Forgotten Bottom?

LR: Well, it was not called the Forgotten Bottom then, it was called Grays Ferry. The Forgotten Bottom is only about five years old. What I attribute to my young years is the play area and all of us that knew each other and we were more friendly as kids. Growing up we did not have any type of violence. We just liked each other. We all just played games together—the boys along with the girls. It took a long time in my lifetime—until I became grown and moved to about ten blocks away from where I was born—that I found out I was poor. The whole community in Grays Ferry—we never realized that we were poor because everyone had just about what everyone had and there were no rich people living next door to us or somebody that had more than the other down the street. I think that has a lot to do with what is happening today. People that are doing things illegally are accumulating money and they are on the same block with people who can't make it. And when they see all this stuff happening with somebody else they start losing their hope and start trying to do things that are illegal because they want the same thing.

SS: What do you like most about living in the Bottom?

LR: You know what I like about liv-

ber my older brothers and sisters and they went to school together. So we still can converse and we laugh about each other and wonder what they are doing and sometimes when one of them comes around to the neighborhood and they see each other it is a really sparkling thing because they remember so much. So I think the uniqueness of Grays Ferry down across 34th Street which is now called the Forgotten Bottom is unique—period. The crime rate is not high because of this unified effort in this community-oriented place. That is the way communities used to be a long,

"You know what I like about living in the Bottom? It is the unified effort of blacks and whites and how we get along."

ing in the Bottom? It is the unified effort of blacks and whites and how we get along. While we were down there and in the early part of my years we never even knew anything concerning racism. And I just love it. We all just love each other. From generation after generation, they raised their kids there and it is just a rapport. Now that we have older Caucasians down there who remem-

long time ago. And I just thank God for the preservation of those things. I have a house on 31st that is about four or five blocks away. It is still in Grays Ferry but it is four or five blocks on the other side of the expressway, where there are a lot of dissension and people are not as friendly and concerned about each other as it is down in the Forgotten Bottom area. And why I think that

Lillian Ray talking to students from the Community Publishing class, 2002

is— Like I said, everybody is trying to do better than the next person and they still live next door to each other. It is not friendliness; it is more like enviness against each other. Then you have the Caucasians and the African Americans that can't get along. So you only have a handful of people that do not like each other, so what happens is those frictions start and it tries to feed on different things such as disliking and putting one against the other. The whites have and the blacks don't have anything.

You know, that kind of thing.

SS: What kind of people make up what is called the Bottom now?

LR: White. Black. We have Asians. We have all kinds of nationalities— Italian, Jewish, and African American. That area is zoned for business and factories.

SS: Did you ever leave the Bottom and why?

LR: I left the Bottom in 1956. I was living with my mother, I got married and we outgrew that house. We found a two-story house that was on 31st. It took me across the expressway, the Schuylkill expressway. I had to do that for room purposes because, I told you, I have nine children. So that's what made me move. I always had connections and my roots were always there.

SS: How have things changed since you returned to the Bottom?

LR: My life has changed tremendously. My life has changed because while I was up on the other side of 34th I found out that the young people in that area had nothing to do. I find that now down the Bottom too. But up there—because I have so many sons and they have their own friends, there was always a bunch of children in my home. So what had happened was that I was concerned about them and I was not concerned about them being shot or on drugs or anything like that, but I was concerned about them not having so much idle time to do things. The first thing I did was put together a basketball league so that they could start doing some constructive things. And that came up very, very well. It was at 31st and Wharton. Each year we made up a basketball league that consisted of 12 teams. It was really, really

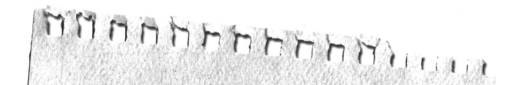

"I always had connections and my roots were always (in the Forgotten Bottom)."

terrific as far as the kids learning how to play sports and being sportsmanlike.

SS: Are any of the children that were playing on the teams still living in that area?

LR: All of them. They are my boys. One thing that happened when I was raising my kids and they had their friends: I always kind of knew that I love them. So they grew up to be men and I just respect them more.

satisfaction for me. Well, anyway, I really wanted a restaurant sometime in my life and this place was available. They called me up and asked me if I was interested in it. My husband had died before that and so I took the money that he had left me and I purchased the house and the store next door. The house is there for me to watch the store. The store is going to be named after my husband. His name was Melvin and the name of the store is going to be

"The best thing that I know that has made me compassionate

SS: On the [class tour of the neighborhood] you stated that you were going to purchase a building. How did you come about getting that building? How do you think it is going to enhance this sense of community in the Bottom?

LR: Well, I always wanted a restaurant—that that was my dream because when I was younger I always liked to cook. My mother used to always cook: she used to sell dinners and I learned from her how to cook. And I don't mind cooking. And I think that came from me liking to cook and when I had all these children it just enhanced my cooking. But just to see the outcome of everyone enjoying it is the

called Melee's. And how will it enhance the community? Well, we are going to sell sandwiches—food for lunch and breakfast. I told you it was in an industrial area but the main thing is that down at the Bottom we have to go four or five blocks in order to get a loaf of bread. So some of the items that we are going to sell are the necessities like toilet tissue, something that they might run out of unexpectedly like paper towels, quarts of milk, and bread. Those are the kinds of groceries that I am going to sell. I am not a grocery store, I am a restaurant. We are going to stay open late to the point when they can at least get something to eat until about ten o'clock at night. There is nothing open, nothing but the bar. And everyone don't want to go in there.

SS: How did you feel about living in the Bottom during the time of the racial incidents that occurred?

LR: At that time I was working for the city and I was assisting Deputy Mayor Ed Rendell. And because I lived down there when all this ruckus was starting he told me to keep my pulse on it. It was always a

the whites who had a structured community center and they had their faults because they were biased—there were no blacks involved. So then you have this handful of African Americans and they were looking at these people as if they were taking everything and not sharing because they were African Americans. Things clashed. It was just like a time bomb with those two organizations and all they were doing was waiting for some-

is that I know that God has blessed me with nine children."

neighborhood that would flare up with different things and there were a few people that were disenfranchised, not able to use their own gifts and making it themselves as opposed to somebody giving it to them. So if they seen someone else achieving something they just automatically assumed that somebody gave it to them, instead of just saying that maybe they worked for what they got, maybe they did something to get what they had. Instead of just sitting around looking at somebody blaming people for their outcome because your hope is gone, because you are not trying to achieve or use your gift. So we have a couple pockets like that. We had

thing to happen, some type of issue, so they can flare up and that is what happened in this race riot stuff. One lady was supposed to have gotten pushed by a Caucasian.

SS: Do you remember if there was a community meeting discussing the issues so that the people could get back together?

LR: Yes I do, and I called that meeting myself. I called the meeting because I knew that it was only two groups involved in this race riot and I knew that there were other organizations such as one that I had called Stinger Square Community Services and Mrs. Riley's First and Last [Center, an intergenerational after-school program] and a whole lot of

"But when it got to me, because of the love I have for my boys, I was pleading with him about the concerns of the boys and how they are not bad and all they need is someone to love them."

other people had organizations out there. So what I did was I sent letters out and called them up and told them after the riot, which was supposed to have happened on that Monday. I called the meeting for that Wednesday. There was ten groups and I told them that you have to have a meeting so we can start to heal our community. Well, out of the ten groups, eight came and we sat and we talked about it. The Forgotten Bottom was not named then. It was just concerned people that came up.

SS: Where was the meeting held?

LR: It was held on 31st Street. When I called them, I just told them it was time for us to heal our community. I told them why I called them—because I knew that everyone was filled with this hatred stuff. So they agreed and from that meeting we just went on and on. We started enhancing each other's programs. So we got the name put together called Grays Ferry Unified.

It consisted of the eight groups that we had; every time we had a meeting we invited the two bickering groups. One said they would not be in the same room as the other, that kind of stuff. I knew that we had to go on, not for anybody's benefit, but for our neighborhood and for our kids so that they can have a close relationship and grow up. So that is what we did and it became very, very good. We had shirts made and we had a Unified picnic every year. People came from all over, young and old. It was held in this great big lot. Everyone had a table—if they wanted to sell cakes. We had a big stage for entertainment.

SS: Where was the lot?

LR: The lot was in the 1200 block of 31st Street, across the street from where I lived.

SS: So how did you get the word out so that people could come?

LR: I worked for the city and I used my people and the mechanisms that I had—I invited some political people to come.

SS: Can you tell me a little bit about your occupation and what it entails?

LR: Well, in 1989, W. Wilson [Goode], who was the Mayor, and I was in the community and I seen this influxuation of drugs and I did not know what drugs was. But I seen a difference in the community that was about to happen. A lady got shot out here and the whole neighborhood was in an uproar. They had a community meeting and it was held at Bishop Newman Church. We all went as a group. Like my Stinger Square Community Services—we went as a group, and when we got there we found out that the Mayor was coming. The Mayor came and he was concerned. It got so out of hand because, you know, it is always like a keg of nails in Grays Ferry, anyway. So this was a white woman that was shot by a black guy. So the whole meeting was just a mess. What he did at the meeting was to say, "Listen, I will pick one person out of each group to come to my office." And that is what he did. So when we met in his office we all had different things that we talked about that we were concerned with. But when it got to me, because of the love I have for my boys, I was pleading with him about the concerns of the boys and how they are not bad and all they need is someone to love them. So a little tear just came out my eye because I felt it very much. To make a long story short, we had about 18 meetings at his office a certain time every month and we came to express the different things that was down in our community. It was more like a unified, organized

"My mom showed us a lot of love. . . .

[She] always had a thing about her that

she made strong women. Her daughters

were strong. We were never ones that

would wait for barriers to come."

thing. From those meetings came the idea to the Mayor to have a Drug Czar. So he took a deputy commissioner of police, Commissioner Armstrong, and he made him the first Drug Czar. Well, him and his smartness, W. Wilson Goode, he knew that he needed to have a community person with him. So out of the 18 people that represented the community, he had us to come in one Saturday, and he said, "I need your help. I need three names that you as a group will nominate for the assistant to the Drug Czar." I never even knew that somebody had nominated me. They sent us out the room and they brought us in one at a time. Told us, what would you do, such and such. To make a long story short, when Wilson Goode came back into the office they gave him the sheet of who they nominated. So it was almost six weeks before—I did not even know that I was getting interviewed when I went to see him—he sent for me. He had all these piles of papers in front of him and I was sitting down talking to him. I was so naive that I did not even realize that he said, "Is there anything in

Melee's Luncheonette, owned and operated by Mrs. Lillian Ray, 2002

your family that I should know about?" So I said that two of my sons have been on drugs, so me and my naive self— He said "Make sure you say that when you go out to speak." So when I was walking out the door all I could remember was "make sure I say that when I go out to speak," but I ain't telling nobody that these boys were on drugs. When I heard him say "make sure you say it when you go out to speak" I did not know I had the job and that I was going out there to speak on his behalf. So we had a meeting and he announced that the assistant to the Drug Czar was going to be Lillian Ray.

SS: You speak very passionately about your activities dealing with the community and children as a whole. Do you think it comes from your upbringing, from what your parents instilled?

LR: Well, my mom showed us a lot of love but it was not that I grew up without a dad. But my mom always had a thing about her that she made strong women. Her daughters were strong. We were never ones that would wait for barriers to come. She was always somebody that supports and took care of her children, and we learned that strength from her. The best thing that I know that has made me compassionate is that I know that God has blessed me with nine children. When I got married I just thought that it was my role as far as not having children, but just being a housewife. The whole doll scenario, playing with the dolls in the house—that was me. And in doing that I learned how to love my children very much. §

Elizabeth Rhodes

Mrs. Elizabeth Rhodes, in front of her house, 2002

Mrs. Elizabeth Rhodes is an 87-year-old woman who is so active she has to plan weeks ahead of time. She is a member of William's Temple C.M.E. Church who "visits the sick, serves on the kitchen committee (during funerals), belongs to the floral club, and missionary society." The services she performed as former Committeewoman (for the 36th Ward, 30th Division) have made her a role model for many neighbors in her community. This phenomenal woman has been a citizen in the Forgotten Bottom for nearly seventy years. She has received numerous awards, including some from the City of Philadelphia and from William's Temple C.M.E. Church, for her dedication to her community. Known as "Aunt Lizzie" to her many nieces and nephews, she enjoys cooking soul food, participating in church activities, and giving back to her community.

"MY LIVING HAS NOT BEEN IN VAIN":

INTERVIEW WITH ELIZABETH RHODES

BY MARKIA MCCLENTON

MARKIA MCCLENTON: Good afternoon, Mrs. Rhodes. How are you?

ELIZABETH RHODES: I'm just fine, honey. And you?

MM: Good! I want you to tell me a little about yourself to start off.

ER: Well, I was born and raised in this area. And last Wednesday I celebrated my 87th birthday—

MM: Oh, Happy Birthday!

ER: Thank you. I came from a family with six of us children—three

stayed here, along with my nieces and nephews and what have you. I don't know, I just got to like it.

MM: What do you like about the neighborhood?

ER: Well, I like the togetherness that we have had. But now, it's changing somewhat. Well, we have younger people and a lot of my playmates and what have you. My parents' friends have passed on and some of them living here have moved. By being here so long, I'm

"I feel very grateful at this time that my living hasn't been in vain."

girls and three boys. And we were all raised in this neighborhood. I have a brother that lives up the street—my oldest brother—and he's 91. But my other brothers and sisters moved away after they married. It just so happened that he and I

just somewhat stuck. I've been living in this block near 70 years. So, you see [laughs]? I don't know how I could get adjusted, you know? But for the most, as far as any racial problems, we don't have them here. And I have seen some of the chil-

163

Mrs. Elizabeth Rhodes at a Forgotten Bottom Neighborhood Association meeting, 2002

dren grow up and they have children and what have you and what not. So I just like it.

MM: You said you were born in this area. So were you born in this house?

ER: Not in this house. But I was born, if you noticed, if you came by the expressway, on a street called Warfield Street. I don't know whether you all noticed it when you were here before. If you came down Wharton St. and you passed a pizza parlor—well, that was the street I was born on. And, of course, the expressway came through and the people had to move out.

MM: Are your parents originally from Philadelphia?

ER: No. My parents are from Maryland. Settled right here in this neighborhood. And then my church is in the neighborhood.

MM: What church do you belong to?

ER: I belong to William's Temple C.M.E. Church over here at 31st and Reed St.

MM: Is that also in the Forgotten Bottom or is it in South Philadelphia?

ER: Yes. Well, it's all South Philadelphia but from 25th on back, we call that Grays Ferry. On this side of the expressway, we have labeled that as the Forgotten Bottom. Seemingly, everything like newspapers and circulars and what have you and what not—we never get them [laughs]. So if there's anything like clean up and what have you and what not they never reach our area or our side. We named it the Forgotten Bottom.

MM: How has living here changed your life?

ER: When you say "living here," it hasn't changed my life, as I would say. Well . . . age [laughs].

MM: You said the neighborhood had changed—

ER: Well, for one thing, we have different type of neighbors, younger people, and their ways is just not my ways. And I find that some of the younger children are not what I think they should be.

MM: That's society in general.

ER: Yeah, that's true, but to a certain degree! Now I tell you what I find and I hate is when the summer's coming.

MM: Why?

ER: It's that loud music! I think some of that music is just disgraceful.

MM: Don't you hate it when you can feel the vibrations?

ER: Yes. Yes. Yes. As far as anything else, there hasn't been a problem.

MM: You said you were a member of William's Temple. Are you an active member and, if so, what types of activities do you participate in?

ER: Very active! Well, I belong to the missionary society. In the Baptist church, I'm considered a Deaconess. I visit the sick and I belong to the floral club. When we have funerals I serve on the kitchen committee—we serve the family, and what have you and what not. I guess it has been about 12 years since I have retired from being the committeewoman in this area. This is the 36th Ward and 30th Division. Then we have a little after school program. I go to a center that we call First and Last—we call it "a little peanut butter and jelly." We make peanut butter and jelly for the children when they come out of school. They have several teachers from our school over here at 32nd

Elizabeth Rhodes with friend and neighborhood resident, Eileen Smith

and Reed Street. They come over and tutor the children. I'm just active in the neighborhood.

MM: Well, what types of activities do you participate in?

ER: By being a former committee person, there's no telling what they want to ask me, you know? [laughs] I do various things like registration when the children—well, I say "children"—when the young people reach the age when they want to know what age to vote. I have registration forms and tell them how and where to get their birth certificates. And other things along them lines.

MM: Do you have a job besides all the activities you do or are you retired?

ER: Oh, I'm retired. Yeah, I'm retired.

MM: How many years –

ER: Well, I put in 22 years at Children's Hospital and that was before it moved to where it is now. I worked at 18th and Bainbridge in Central Supply. And after I left Children's Hospital, I called myself retiring and was out about I guess a year and a half before I decided to go back to work at the State building, where I put in nine and a half years. So then, after that, I fully retired.

MM: You mentioned that the chil-

dren these days are different. Do you think it is because they have different traditional values?

ER: Yes. Yes. Yes. The way I see it is children raising children.

MM: True.

ER: It's altogether different from when I was growing up. And some of these children are running the street day and night and what have you and what not. And just free to roam. I guess they have some type of supervision but it doesn't seem like much to me.

MM: What type of work did your parents do?

ER: Domestic and my father was a laborer.

MM: Did you go to school in this neighborhood?

ER: Yes. I went to James Alcorn School. Then it was located at 33rd and Dickinson. Later I went on to . . . uh . . . uh—ain't that awful?— Smith School at 19th and Wharton. And then, I went to Benson.

MM: I heard you like to cook. What types of things do you like to cook?

ER: Food! [laughs]

MM: Well, I know that.

ER: Well, nowadays these girls say they know how to cook when they pop a dinner in the oven or they say they made something when it's already made and all they have to

Williams Temple C.M.E Church, 3133 W. Reed St.

do is put it in the oven. I like to cook from scratch.

MM: Do you make homemade cakes—

ER: And pies. Yes.

MM: You showed me various awards, but how do you feel about receiving all these awards?

ER: I feel very grateful at this time that my living hasn't been in vain.

MM: Has God been a big part of your life?

ER: Yes. I had a Christian mother and father, I was raised in a Christian home. I know no other than to do right. At this age, I know right from wrong [laughs].

MM: Do you think your parents had a lot of—

ER: Sure. Your upbringing. Now, some adults have been brought up right but somewhere along the line, they have strayed. See, it wasn't them that wasn't brought up right but it was them that strayed.

MM: Have you ever strayed in life?

ER: Honey, yes, but to a certain degree. I don't know of anybody that's been good. I mean good good. I don't know of anybody that's been bad—well, too bad. You find some bad people, but through it all, you find some good about them.

MM: What has put you on the right path after you have strayed?

ER: My upbringing.

MM: What do you value the most?

ER: My family. My nieces and nephews—I have beautiful nieces and nephews.

MM: Do all of them live around here?

ER: Not all of them, but some of them. Some of them live in Maryland, New Jersey and Boston.

MM: What inspires you to get up every day and help around your

"You know, years ago, they use to label Methodist people as being cold, where Baptist people get emotional. We're not as cold as people label us to be."

neighborhood and your community?

ER: I just want to be available and I just want to be of service to people the best that I can. I think that it's so much we can do so, I can't find the time to just sit up in here to just watch TV all day.

MM: You're a busy lady.

ER: Honey, I go out everyday! Every day I have something to do. I try to plan my week.

MM: Well, if you have to plan your week that means you have a lot to do.

ER: That's right, yes indeed. I'm not one to sit in the house. I rise early and do all I can do before 10:30, 11 a.m. And that's it for the rest of the day, 'cause I'm gone. I like to get out, I like to socialize, I like to go to movies, and I like plays.

MM: Have you seen any lately?

ER: I'm going up with a group from the church to see "Daniel."

MM: Does your church give back to the community?

ER: On Wednesdays at our church, we have Bible study and a soup kitchen and that's free for everybody that wants to come.

MM: How does William's Temple

benefit the neighborhood?

ER: It opens up to let people have fellowship. If they don't know anyone, they have the opportunity to socialize. I usually see most of the younger folks that get to socialize. You get to know folks—I think that's nice.

Williams Temple church members with Reverend Elton Woodard, 1945

MM: What kind of atmosphere does your church offer? Is it one of those Holy Ghost churches or is it more laid back?

ER: No, it's not a laid-back church. You know, years ago, they use to label Methodist people as being cold, where Baptist people get emotional. We're not as cold as people label us to be. We have a fine young minister and he likes to include many of the young people in various things. When I was coming up, you had to sit up in church and be quiet. But now young people are taking charge and becoming more active in the church. For instance, we have two groups of praise dancers and that has brought quite a few young people in. Seemingly, the girls are between the ages of 14 and 18. They have friends that they bring to church. The pastor also is starting a computer class for the young people. I think it's nice.

MM: That's wonderful because not every church gives back to the community.

ER: I think that's the purpose of a church in the neighborhood.

MM: What makes this neighborhood so different from other ones? Why is the Forgotten Bottom so special?

ER: When you say "the Forgotten Bottom," on this end of 34th St. we have peace and harmony. Now on the other side, maybe you've read about the racial tensions?

MM: Yes, I heard about it.

ER: Yeah, we don't have that down here! We have the black and the white and we live together. I don't know of any time we've ever had those kind of problems.

MM: Why do you think it's like that?

ER: It's the people.

MM: I'm sure that there are people from your generation on the other side as well.

ER: It's about respecting others.

MM: Does everybody respect one another in this neighborhood?

ER: Yes.

MM: Would you consider yourself a lucky person?

ER: Very fortunate, honey. I'm still able to get around and do for myself. I guess I still got my wits about me to the extent that I can handle my own business. I'm in a reasonable portion of health. My biggest problem is my pressure. If I'd eat right . . . [laughs].

MM: Maybe it because of the things you cook!

ER: Yeah, that's it. Like I said, I'm fortunate at this age to have a good appetite. If I ate right, I could control my pressure.

MM: What kind of food do you cook?

ER: Greens, cabbage, cornbread, fish, chicken—

MM: Just your average soul food?

ER: You got it [laughs]. There's nothing like homemade cooking. I make my own soup. Campbell's tastes good but sometimes I can put them to shame! [laughs]

MM: So Campbell's does good, but Mrs. Rhodes does best?

ER: I don't know why they don't have me canning my soup. I like food. I used to do a lot of entertaining and that just calls for food.

You young folks don't have to carry on like we did. If you want greens or something you can get a package of greens.

MM: Not me. I know how to cook. My mom knows how to cook, but my grandmother doesn't. But my grandmother makes mean soups and salads. My mom makes Spanish food, soul food, whatever. But, she didn't always know how to cook. I was brought up on pork and beans, oatmeal, and stuff like that.

ER: No kidding. How large is your family?

MM: Pretty big. Most of my family is dispersed throughout the United States. I live with my mom and my grandmom lives about 5 minutes away.

ER: You're fortunate.

MM: I know. I have a good family. My family and friends are also my cherished possessions.

ER: I have lovely friends and beautiful friends. In order to get a friend you have to be a friend—that's just the way I feel. [Mrs. Rhodes shows some of her awards.] These are the various awards I have received. I try to make my living not in vain so I do the best I can.

MM: One of your awards mentioned something about the Eastern Stars—are you an Eastern Star? My grandmother is one.

ER: Yeah? What chapter is she in? I have been a Star going on 52 years.

MM: I don't know—she's not active anymore. She's from South Philly. My grandmother's maiden name was Lillian Stokes. She's a member of the Stokes family—they owned a flower shop.

ER: Yes! They lived over there at 34th.

MM: I'm trying to think of what my great-grandfather's name was.

ER: Was it Charlie Gaines?

MM: No, his last name was Stokes.

ER: Yeah, they had the flower shop. You have an aunt or somebody by the name of Ina?

MM: No, their names were Vivian, Lillian, Charlotte, Linda, Rita, Kathy—

ER: I know them. They lived over there at 32nd and Dickinson St.

MM: I know they lived on the other side of Grays Ferry. My great-grandmother's name was Vivian.

ER: That's going back some years. Honey, you got me cookin' now. They owned until they started building the expressway and then they had to move out.

MM: There were so many of them. My grandmother Lillian looks just like my great-grandmother Vivian. And I have an aunt named Vivian. There were 8 girls and 6 boys—

ER: I don't remember the males,

but I do remember the Stokes girls—that's what they were called. One of them died over there too.

MM: No, my Aunt Kay was the only daughter that died and she didn't die until about 5 years ago. Her maiden name was Vivian Kay Stokes. Later she married and became Vivian Kay Dillahay, but she went by Kay. She was also an Eastern Star.

ER: She belonged to my chapter. [Mrs. Rhodes showed me the names of my Aunt Kay and great-grandfather in her Eastern Star directory]. She was our past matron. Isn't this something? See what I'm talking about?

MM: It's a small world—

ER: Honey, you have to be careful how you treat people. You never know in life who you're gonna meet. It pays to treat people right.

MM: You know so much about my family.

ER: Now, it must have been somebody over there—your great-grandmother—that was sick.

MM: That would have to be my great-grandmother because she died kind of young.

ER: [laughs] If this ain't something!

MM: God works in mysterious ways! I remembered meeting you at the meeting and something told me to interview you.

ER: I knew the Stokes. Now, like I said, Vivian was my past matron.

MM: What exactly is a matron?

ER: It's something like a . . . well, I'll let them tell you because it's a secret order. Now, I'll be sitting here thinking because that wasn't yesterday. I remember the Stokes, but only a very few people around here would remember the Stokes.

MM: I guess it's because they didn't stay as long—

ER: It's not that—we have more people, see! My brother and I are the oldest two people in this block. Other people would remember the flower shop, but not like I would because I'm older. A lot of people know I have a lot of nieces and nephews and they call me Aunt Lizzie. I tell them, let people know how I come to be an aunt. I used to call my mother's friends "aunt," but they weren't my mother's or father's sisters. It's just a title, but I say, tell the children. You have all these young women having babies out of wedlock and then they have all these brothers and sisters scattered all around. Let 'em know who they are.

MM: Yeah, because you never know who you'll come across.

ER: That's right.

MM: Do you have any children?

ER: No, I don't have any children

but I have so many nieces and nephews you'd think I did [laughs]. Now, one of my older nephews refers to me as "Mom" and one of my great-great nephews calls me "Grandmom."

MM: Are you still an active Star? If so, do you go to meetings?

ER: There are young girls at the lodge now. I'm past all of that now. I don't attend meetings like I used to years ago. It's not that I'm disinterested, but times have changed. You used to be able to get on a bus after a meeting, but you can't do that anymore in the nighttime. And I don't drive.

MM: Did you ever learn how to drive?

ER: No. But my nephews tell me I don't need a car 'cause I can get one of them to take me somewhere [laughs]. That's another thing I have seen change—

MM: What?

ER: The times we are living in. Just the other day we were coming from church on Wednesday. We were going to a young lady's home at 54th and Spruce. We were driving on 37th and Walnut Street and we seen policemen, sirens were going, and police cars were coming from every direction. When we got to 52nd Street—Oh my good Lord, then we knew something was going on. That night, I heard on the news that a boy had called in a bomb threat for the El. When the police got the bomb threat they shut the trains down. By 9 o'clock that night they had traced the boy through his cell phone [laughs]. Now, we did some stupid things in my time but not like that.

MM: It's a shame. People have lost their values.

ER: Now, when I was coming along, if a girl had a baby she was an outcast. But now it's a common

"A little girl down the street called me 'Elizabeth' and I said, 'Who told you to call me that?' And you know what she said? She said, 'Ain't that your name?' So then I told her what to call me and she called me 'Mrs. Elizabeth' from then on in.

thing. I remember I was on the bus one day, and a group of young girls got on the bus with babies. Later that day, I called my sister and I asked her if she knew where they could have been going. She said they were probably going to school, since they have day cares in the schools now. I've also noticed young people referring to older people by their name, but that's being disrespectful to me. I call some of the younger ones "Mr." and "Miss" and I'm old enough to be some of their grandmothers. A little girl down the street called me "Elizabeth" and I said, "Who told you to call me that?" And you know what she said? She said, "Ain't that your name?" So then I told her what to call me and she called me "Mrs. Elizabeth" from then on in.

MM: I really appreciate you doing this interview with me. Thank you very much.

ER: Oh honey, it's my pleasure. §

Alice Riley

Photo: John Edward Jordan

Mrs. Alice L. Riley

Mrs. Alice Riley is a resident of Grays Ferry, Philadelphia. She has lived just a few short blocks from the Forgotten Bottom her entire life. Mrs. Riley has been a member of Williams Temple C.M.E Church since she was a young child. She has three children, two sons, and one daughter, and is the grandmother of four. A community-oriented person who developed her values from her faith and sense of family, Mrs. Riley's love for the people of her community is exemplified in the center she opened in 1983. She was inspired to start The First and Last Center to promote relationships between young people and senior citizens, and to provide activities to enrich the lives of the children in her community. She also raised a foster daughter, Rosetta, for 14 years, who now has two children.

"FIRST AND LAST":

AN INTERVIEW WITH ALICE L. RILEY

BY TIFFANY PATTERSON

TIFFANY PATTERSON: Can you tell me what year you were born?

ALICE RILEY: 1931.

TP: And you were born in "The Bottom," right in this neighborhood that we—

AR: No, I was born two blocks down the expressway. The expressway is on 34th Street.

TP: Can you tell me what type of work your parents did?

AR: My mother was a homemaker. My father, he worked at— Well, my father died when I was three. But my stepfather worked at Dupont, just a couple blocks down from here.

TP: Is that still open now?

AR: Yeah, they are still open.

TP: Were you educated as a child?

AR: Yes, I graduated from high school in 1949.

TP: Can you tell me what schools you went to?

AR: James Alcorn Elementary School, Audenreid Junior High and William Penn High School for Girls.

TP: What church do you go to?

AR: Williams Temple C.M.E Church.

TP: Can you tell me about some of the values your parents taught you? Were you a strictly religious family?

AR: No. Well, not overbearing, but they always taught us respect for ourselves and for other people. We had to attend Sunday school and church or we couldn't go anywhere else. We had a large family. We went to the neighborhood movie theater or played with other children in the area. It wasn't overbearing, but you had to respect others and adults were allowed to correct you, which is not allowed these days.

TP: Yeah.

AR: [laughs] It's more like . . . well . . . they were kind of like your parents when your parents weren't available.

TP: So it was definitely like a sense of community?

Children at Alcorn School, 1981

AR: Yes, very tight community.

TP: Can you tell me about your first love?

AR: My first what?

TP: Love.

AR: [laughs] First love. What do you want to know about him?

TP: How you met, how long you were together, if you're still together.

AR: We met through church.

TP: Can you tell me his name?

AR: His name was Arthur Isaacs—he's dead now, but that's not the person I married.

TP: Can you tell me about your husband?

AR: I met him through my brother—they worked together. At the beginning I wasn't looking for a relationship because I was 17.

Eventually, he kept talking to me and so forth, so we got engaged after about six months and we got married in about a year.

TP: How long have you been married?

AR: Well, I was married 29 years, I'm divorced now.

TP: Oh, really. Do you feel comfortable talking about the divorce?

AR: What do you want to know?

TP: Do you think you know why it didn't work out? I mean, 29 years is a long time.

AR: Yeah, it is long time, but I was more of a family person and he was not.

TP: Do you think you grew apart over the years?

AR: Yes, I was into church. When we were going together he would attend but when we got married he didn't want to attend anymore, so that was a break right then. He supported me, but I would have preferred if he had been in church and participated in the same things that I did.

TP: Tell me about your children.

AR: I have three. My oldest son's name is Thomas—he lives in New Jersey. He works for Pepsi Cola Company—he went there straight out of college and he's an administrator there. He has one son, Corey, graduated from Princeton—now he's a trader on Wall Street. My second son's name is Bruce. He has a very bad back and is semi-disabled. He has a beautiful voice and loves to sing. He lives with me and helps me out a lot. My daughter Karen lives in New Castle, Delaware. She has three children. She graduated high school and she's working on her AA in child development. She's what they call a paraprofessional.

TP: You said you met your husband through your brothers. How many brothers do you have?

AR: I had eight, but I only have one now.

TP: Did you have any sisters?

AR: Well, I have two stepsisters and one half sister.

TP: Did you find it difficult growing up in a household with so many children?

AR: Since I was the only girl, for awhile I had my mother to myself. When she married my stepfather he already had two girls and later they had another girl together, so then I had other girls I could relate to in the family.

TP: Were you friends with your stepfather?

AR: Yes. He was really the only

Mrs. Riley's parents, Charles and Lula Nixon, 1940s

father I knew. Only thing I remember about my father was when they were taking him to the hospital. They came back and said that he had died, so I really don't remember anything at all about him.

TP: So can you tell me about the First and Last Center?

AR: My brother and I organized this program in 1983 because there were no activities in this area for youth or senior citizens. We started tutoring kids in reading right outside my home, which is one block down 32nd St. Our first volunteers were my daughter, Karen, a young neighbor, Valerie Jones, and my best friend, Lillian Henley. We did that until we got [this building.] We've been here since 1986. We work with the youth after-school program, summer program, and we have a ceramics class for senior citizens and we also take them on trips.

TP: How many children are in the program?

AR: It's an average of 45.

TP: You worked at the schools for many years, I've been told.

AR: Yes, 27 years. Before that I worked at the Federal Government Naval Department for 14 years.

TP: And were you a teacher when you worked in the schools?

AR: School Secretary.

TP: Secretary. So do you like working with kids?

AR: Oh, yeah. I've been active with children since 1952. I started working with the youth choir at the church.

TP: Can you tell me what it is about children—why you like working with them?

Alice Moore Riley, graduation from William Penn High School for Girls, 1949

AR: I like to see them achieve, especially children who are underserved, who have problems, children who are neglected. I work with all of them, but I am especially drawn to the children others may overlook.

TP: Over the 27 years what schools did you work in?

AR: Well, several. The last school that I retired from was James Alcorn, same school I went to when I was a kid.

TP: Can you tell me the racial makeup of the school?

"I think the teachers are paid very well, but the problem is the discipline. . . . So it's just too many disruptions in the classroom for the teacher to effectively teach. Some of them do a good job and some of them can't handle it."

AR: When I was working there, at least—85% black, and maybe 10% white, and 5% Oriental. Now it's just about maybe 95% black and the others are Oriental. I don't think there are any white kids there at all.

TP: Over the years of working at the school and working with the children, have you seen any changes in the children—do they have any more behavioral problems?

AR: They've regressed—well, in every phase that I can see, the behavior's horrible. Of course, when they come here I have certain standards they have to follow or else they are not allowed to stay in the program. But I also run the school store at Alcorn School and I see how they act. Like, in the lunchroom they are disrespectful to the adults and they're just, like, wild. They run all around and play on the floor—these are like, fifth grade to eighth grade. Up at the main building they have kindergarten to fourth grade. But they seem to be so hyper, and mainly, I think, it's because they have young parents who never had a childhood themselves because they've been raising kids and they don't give them enough attention.

TP: Do you see the problems in the schools itself not enforcing rules? Teachers feeling overwhelmed?

AR: Sure, they are afraid of the kids. The kids go home and tell their parents and the parents don't come up with the right attitude. They have a bad attitude and they're ready to fight and they chastise the teachers in front of the children, so the kids feel they can do that too.

TP: Yeah.

AR: Yes, if the parents don't show respect, the kids don't show respect.

TP: With the children do you see a lot of involvement from the parents?

AR: Nope. It's hard getting some of them to even volunteer or attend meetings.

" . . . I went to visit a cousin in Baltimore and they had this big shopping area and we went down there and I had to go to the bathroom. That was the first I ever saw a sign that said 'For Colored Only.' I called my mother and told her I wanted to come home."

TP: So when you were a secretary at the school did you interact with children a lot?

AR: Yes, all the time. I was the first one the kids saw. I registered them for school and took care of the school business.

TP: Were most of the children that you saw a discipline problem?

AR: I saw all kinds of kids. The kids who got in trouble went to the administrator, who would be available to take care of them. Of course, I did get some of them, you know. Now they don't come down to the office—they go to the accommodation room, but that's only been in the last 3 or 4 years.

TP: Do you see a problem between the amount of money teachers are paid and their performance? Do you think that if they receive pay increases they would be able to perform better or be better teachers?

AR: No, I think the teachers are paid very well, but the problem is the discipline. One or two kids could spoil it for the whole class. And corporal punishment is out the window, you know that. So it's just too many disruptions in the classroom for the teacher to effectively teach. Some of them do a good job and some of them can't handle it. What I do see, I think, it's easier for the black teachers than for the white teachers because they have students who call the white teachers names. The white teachers have a tendency to be afraid of the parents and the black teachers aren't.

TP: Do you think it's because the children and the parents of the children see the black teachers as more on their level, as far as, because they're black they see them as—

AR: Not only on their level just because the fact that they're black.

Some of the black teachers have problems with black parents too. But I think it's the fact that they're black and a lot of them are young and they don't want white teachers telling their kids what to do.

TP: Do you think that overall Philadelphia schools get a bad rap?

AR: Yes, I do.

TP: Do you think they are better schools than people say they are or they could use an improvement?

AR: I think they are better. If the parents don't come in the building they don't know what's going on. They only go by what they hear. At Alcorn they have about 1100-1200 kids enrolled between the two schools and at the school meeting they'll have about six parents. They show no interest in the kids. Now, if the kids are going to be performing on stage, or something like that, they will come out.

TP: But, as far as academics, they're not concerned.

AR: They're not concerned. They're not interested. They don't even come to pick up the kids from school. Now not all, but there's a majority that don't show interest at all. I think it's mostly the young parents who have children at such a young age and have really missed their own childhoods. Now they want to do the things they missed.

They now have the responsibility of raising children themselves, but they can't handle it.

TP: Because they don't know how to be parents themselves.

AR: Right, right.

TP: Have you personally faced racial problems or come across discrimination because of your color or because you are a woman?

AR: No, not— Maybe when I was a kid, not since I've been an adult. I remember this instance at Alcorn School where I wanted to be the messenger and the teacher would always call on this white girl to be the messenger. I remember that specifically, but no, I haven't experienced any racial problems.

TP: Do you think it's because you grew up in Philadelphia that you

Enoch Norris, Mrs. Riley's cousin, 1950s

wouldn't see it as discrimination?

AR: Probably so. One instance I remember, not racial discrimination, but I went to visit a cousin in Baltimore and they had this big shopping area and we went down there and I had to go to the bathroom. That was the first I ever saw a sign that said "For Colored Only."

TP: Really?

AR: I called my mother and told her I wanted to come home. But that's really all that I've seen. I guess that's because I was raised around black people.

TP: What is it that you think is so special about the neighborhood?

AR: The people seem to care about each other, are there for each other, are concerned for each other. They try to keep the neighborhood clean. They're friendly and it's a rather quiet neighborhood. They don't have fighting and things like that. Even the younger people—they seem to respect the older people, they look out for us.

TP: The racial tensions that were occurring in Grays Ferry, it seemed not to spill over into the Bottom.

AR: No, I don't think it came no further than 31st St.

TP: Can you tell me why you think it didn't affect you or—

AR: For one thing, I don't like controversy. I try to keep it as far away from me as I can and then I try to look into why it happened, and then I try to go on from there. If I thought it was unjust I might give my opinion, but I just don't like controversy. Older people don't like— It's mostly the young crowd, with that type of behavior.

TP: Hasn't Grays Ferry had a long history of racial tensions?

AR: Yes, from 30th St. east, but I just don't go into that area unless I'm driving through. When we were kids we had a spat every now and

"People in the Northeast—they don't know anything about South Philadelphia. . . . It would be good for some of the white population to know that not all blacks are stupid and ignorant and not that they don't have decent places to live and don't have jobs, but they don't know it's a lot of good people. Me being one."

then, but it wasn't— It was no big deal to me. My mother always told me, If somebody don't want to be bothered with you, don't bother with them. You know.

TP: Yes.

AR: You don't have to sit or live around white people to make yourself feel important.

TP: What do you feel brings you importance?

AR: With people? I take each person as an individual. I don't like to group people together. Somebody might tell me something about you, but I don't accept it until I talk to you, until I see you. If you haven't done anything, it's all right with me. The most important thing is that they have good values.

TP: Can you tell me what you consider good values?

AR: If they're a student, they should be going to school.

TP: Yes.

AR: They shouldn't be going around cursing and carrying on. Keep themselves presentable and girls should dress like young ladies and act like young ladies. If possible, they should be a member of a church because they learn a lot of their values there. They should be responsible in taking care of the property they have and wherever it is they live, in a house, apartment.

Riley children, 1959

They should be helpful to their parents. They should be respectful. This is stuff that is just normal with me. And, of course, I expect everybody else to do the same thing and that doesn't always happen, but that's what I expect.

TP: Is there anything else you wanted to tell?

AR: No. Just that it's a good idea that Temple is embarking on this [project] and trying to find out about a neighborhood, so that other people will know about it. People in the Northeast—they don't know anything about South Philadelphia. They never heard of the Forgotten Bottom. A lot of people have only heard of Grays Ferry 'cause of the incidents they had here. That's the only thing. They don't know about the good things that are going on around here. One rotten apple spoils the whole bunch. You need to

State Representative Harold James presenting a grant to Alice C. Riley for First and Last

come down and see something, like this [book] that you are going to produce. It's a lot of good things going on down here, a lot of good people. It would be good for some of the white population to know that not all Blacks are stupid and ignorant and not that they don't have decent places to live and don't have jobs, but they don't know it's a lot of good people. Me being one. §

Dedication of Mural "Guardian Angels" (painted by Jason Slowik and Eric Okdeh) on wall next to Williams Temple CME, 32nd and Reed.

Christine Rivello

Christine Rivello with her father, Romeo, 2002

C hristine Rivello was born 43 years ago and grew up on Grove St. At one time, she had so many relatives living in the immediate area that the street was known as "Rivello St." She was one of five children. She went to school at King of Peace and St. Gabriel's and left school to take a job at the old Wanamakers Department Store at 13th and Market. Since that time, she has worked at a number of jobs around the city, mostly waitressing. She has remained an active member of the Forgotten Bottom community and lives around the corner from her parents on 36th St. with her son, "Little Romeo," and her husband.

"KISSING IN THE CABOOSES":

AN INTERVIEW WITH CHRISTINE RIVELLO

BY SUSAN B. HYATT

SUSAN HYATT: What are your best memories about growing up here?

CHRISTINE RIVELLO: Well, I was born and raised on Grove Street 43 years ago. When I was growing up there, Grove Street was almost all Rivellos! My father [Romeo Rivello] was one of 14 kids and we had all of his brothers and sisters living near us. All around us were my cousins and all—so it was fun, really. We all grew up together. The Wests were our Black neighbors and they grew up with us, too. My dad is a good man —he's the best. All the young guys always liked my father. Well, they still do—a lot of them still live around here. He really misses the Italian club we used to have up here. It's a Black club now. Every Sunday, all the guys would come around to see my father. They had a lot of respect for my father.

SH: Are you the only one of the kids still living in this neighbor-hood?

CR: Yeah, the other ones didn't want to come back. When I was growing up, we had all the cousins and the aunts and uncles plus my grandparents, we used to get together at my grandmother's to have pastine.

SH: What's pastine?

CH: It's a chicken soup with little tiny round bits of pasta. What, you've never had pastine?

SH: I don't think so!

CR: We used to eat it with 12, 13 kids around the table. We had it every day for lunch. Sometimes we had raviolis. We had a large family. All the cousins, we all knew each other's friends because we were all around the same age—a couple years here, a couple years there—

SH: What were some of the great traditions you had when you were growing up on "Rivello Street"?

CR: We had all the holidays togeth-er—Christmas Eve was the biggest.

"Once in awhile, the cows would get out from the meat

> "One year, the night before Christmas Eve, my father stayed out a little too late with the guys and they came home and ate all the fish my mother'd made for Christmas Eve! I'll never forget it as long as I live—that was the year we had to order pizza for Christmas Eve!"

We always had fish on Christmas Eve. All our friends would come around—my father's buddies from GE would come over. Our house, it was like it had a revolving door—everyone was always in and out, in and out. One year, the night before Christmas Eve, my father stayed out a little too late with the guys and they came home and ate all the fish my mother'd made for Christmas Eve! I'll never forget it as long as I live—that was the year we had to order pizza for Christmas Eve! My mother was having a fit.

SH: What church did you go to?

CR: St. Gabriel's [at 26th and Dickinson].

SH: What school did you go to?

CR: I went to King of Peace first. But I was a bad kid. Me and my cousin Darlene, we were like partners in crime. We weren't that bad, but we used to drive the nuns crazy and all. Then I went to St. Gabe's. I didn't graduate from high school—I got my GED. I had a job right after I left school. I worked at Wanamaker's [Department Store]. All of my brothers and my sister—I have 3 brothers and one sister—we all went to work. We always earned money. When I was a kid, on Saturday morning, I'd get up and get my little bucket of water and my scrub brush, and I used to scrub everyone's front steps on Grove St. for them. They used to give me a nickel and before I knew it, I'd have about $10. I used to baby-sit, there was this old lady and I used to clean her house. I used to scrub old ladies' kitchen floors, for dollar or a quar-

house and we'd chase them down the street. Whole truckloads!"

ter or whatever they'd give me. We all knew how to hustle, we did. We all made our money. My brothers used to work as shoeshine guys on the corner. There was a real good bar on the corner; my uncle used to bartend there. That was in the days when everyone wore shoes and not sneakers. They used to make a good penny doing that!

SH: What do you miss most about the old neighborhood?

CR: In the hot weather, we used to sleep outside—you didn't have to worry about anything.

SH: You mean in the park?

CR: No, right out front—right on the pavement in a lounge chair! I still like to sit out there and fall asleep. I still know just about everybody in the neighborhood—except for some of the Chinese who've moved in. Most of the other people in the neighborhood were born and raised around here. Annie, she's still one of my best friends. And Karen, she still lives around here. I'll tell you what I miss most, though: when we were 13, 14—there used to be so many guys around here. Because we had factories all around us—we had Barrett's, we had DuPont, Celetex, Oscar Meyer— there must have been four guys to every one girl! And Carter's, where Bessie's Chicken Shack is now. From early in the morning, you used to be able to smell the pizza . . . there used to be lines all down the block! The whole neighborhood used to get in line waiting to get a slice of that pizza. And they used to have water ice. We used to put vodka shots in the water ice and no one knew what we were drinking! And we used to go up to the slaughterhouse—we used to get a kick out of it, watching the animals get killed. Once in awhile, the cows would get out from the meat house and we'd chase them down the street. Whole truckloads! Now it's much quieter—you could hear a pin drop. We used to get guys who'd come down here from 29th Street. You know how it is, we were young. There were no drugs then. We'd smoke cigarettes, though. My father caught me once and made me eat one on the corner! In front of everyone—I was so embarrassed! I was about 12 at the time. I always used to be able to con my father— even when he'd punish me, I'd say, "Please, Dad, please, Dad—I'll never do it again!" I'm next to the youngest. I'm still afraid of my father—well, not afraid, exactly, but I still respect him.

SH: Can you tell me a little about the history of the club across the street, St. John's?

CR: I don't actually know that much about St. John's. From what I know, it used to be a Polish club. I think the original owner went bankrupt and someone else took it over. What I really remember is the Italian club that we used to have at 35th and Wharton. That's the one my father used to go to. He was a steward, he used to go to that club for years. I remember they used to have Halloween parties every year – you know, for the older people. My mother and father, they used to get all dressed up. I remember one year, my aunt scared me so bad! I can't remember exactly what she was dressed as but she was so scary. My aunt, she used to be awesome. My Aunt Juliet? We had Romeo and Juliet! One year, she dressed as Phyllis Diller! She was identical—it was hilarious. They used to have a lot of entertainment up there. We couldn't wait until the New Year's Eve party. They used to have these big parties. I remember one year, there were all these guys from the neighborhood and all these girls who weren't from the neighborhood—I guess they were from southwest Philly, not too far away. So I didn't know any of them. We'd have a lookout to see if my mother or my father or any of my aunts were coming down the street, 'cause they'd come to the club, too.

Christine Rivello's first communion

I remember one time when I was 16, I moved out of my house for awhile. I couldn't wait to come back home! My mother did everything for us—I didn't even know how to turn on the washer when I left home. Wash dishes, make our bed—never! My mother did everything, especially for my brothers. One time when I was doing the dishes, I started throwing them in the trash—silverware, everything! Because I couldn't wait to go out— my friends were out on the street, waiting for me. My mom is great, though—she's been through a lot.

SH: I asked her if there'd been any controversy when she married your dad since she was Irish.

CR: No, that wasn't a problem but she converted because she'd been a

> "My mother used to lean out the door and call us all in from the street—I used to be so embarrassed. She'd lean out the door and call, 'Christine Philamena Eileen Rivello!'"

Presbyterian. So she became a Catholic. And my grandmother taught her to make Italian food. My mother makes the best gravy—I don't know why we call it gravy—it's the pasta sauce. On Sunday's, we'd all eat together at around 1:00 in the afternoon. There'd be 13 or 14 of us around the table. We'd have a big dinner—macaroni, everything. When we were kids, my father would make the best jellyrolls ever! He doesn't even remember what goes in them now. We used to have dinner every day at 4:30. My mother used to lean out the door and call us all in from the street—I used to be so embarrassed. She'd lean out the door and call, "Christine Philamena Eileen Rivello!" She'd call us all, using all our middle names. The whole neighborhood would say to me, "Christine, your mother wants you home for dinner!" I know my father and mother had hard times, but we never knew. Like, sometimes we'd run out of coal—

SH: You used to have coal fires?

CR: Oh, yeah, everyone around here had coal! We ran out of coal quite a few times but nobody ever knew it. I didn't even know until I was older and my mother used to tell me these stories. I said, "Get out of here!" I couldn't believe it!

SH: Your mother told me she couldn't believe she'd raised five kids in the house they live in.

CR: They hardly have enough room now and there's only two of them. They accumulate—I moved back there when I was 30. Me and my son, little Romeo, he's 21 now. We moved back for awhile.

SH: For how long?

CR: Well, let's see—my son was 8 months old. I'd left my husband 'cause he was really crazy. They put him in a psychiatric hospital. I guess he took some bad dope or something.

SH: How had you met him?

CR: I was working in this bar at 18th and McKean. I met him there.

I should have listened to my mother! When I brought him over to meet her, she said, "I don't like his shoes." Because he had white shoes on. And, guess what? I should have listened to her because they hated his guts! I guess because he wasn't very polite or anything and he wasn't a very good provider, even when I had the

Christine Rivello, 2002

baby. Then I went back to work. My mother and my sister always used to look after my son—he was always a good baby. My first job was at Wanamaker's—at 13th and Market. You know, where Lord & Taylor is now. I worked there for quite a few years. Since then, I've mostly worked as a waitress. I used to work at Kelly's Seafood—I'll never forget

that. It was at 11th and Chestnut. It was a famous, famous restaurant about 23 years ago. I always had money because I used to make great tips. I'd like to get a real job with benefits and all, though. I don't mind waitressing but there's no benefits. Like medical, but what are you going to do? You can't have everything. I thank God every day. I work, I have a great son. He's in school and he's a mechanic. He's doing great.

SH: How did you meet Andy [her current husband]?

CR: He worked for the railroad. And he looked so lonely! I remember one night, I was coming home from work and he was in the club and he looked so lonely! At that time, I was working at Pizzeria Uno, and I would bring the bartender home a pizza every night. He worked on the railroad about 32 years—he's got a little jump on me in age—I'm 43, he's 67. I looked at him and I thought, "This guy looks lonely." He was just sitting by himself, looking real quiet. Well, I thought he was quiet, anyway. Then I went back in there the next Sunday. My girlfriend was the bartender, her name was Carol, she used to live next door years ago. I wanted to go to the racetrack and she started kicking my leg. There was only me and Andy in the club.

> **"We were coming back [from Atlantic City] and I'm in the back seat, waving the money around like I'm rich! I gave my mother a thousand, my father a thousand, by the time I got home, I only had about four hundred left!"**

And she's kicking me and kicking me! I said, "What are you doing?" She's killing my leg! And she said, "Why don't you invite that guy to go with you?" So that's how we first got hooked up. My leg was black and blue when I finally caught on! And then, I stood him up! We were supposed to go the next day to Philly Park to the racetrack. I got all dressed up—I told my mother. She was watching my son. I walked

A young Christine with her brothers on "Rivello Street," 1960

around the block twice and I got, like, really nervous. I went back home that day and never met him. When I saw him, I gave him some excuse—I told him I had to work. And he said, "No, you didn't have to work—I saw you walking around the block." And I said "That wasn't me," but it was. Then I came home one night, and he was staying at what they used to call the Railroad House—at the end of Reed St. A gentleman bought the house and when the railroad workers used to come up from like Reading or Harrisburg or wherever—they used to work down here like part-time— he used to rent them rooms. And that was that. I've seen my husband every day since then—and that was a long time ago. The best thing I ever did was meet Andy. He has two other kids and a grandson, too. He retired from the railroad after 42 years. He basically raised my son. He's a good guy. Romeo was about seven when we met. He used to take him to baseball games and everything. We used to go out almost every night, we used to dance, we used to have a ball! Everybody loves him—they think he's quiet. He is a good guy. We like to go down to Atlantic City about once a month. We go to the Casino Hotel, have a few margaritas, gamble a bit.

SH: I've never been to Atlantic City.

CR: Oh, you should go! It's really nice. You'll probably have beginner's luck and win! Usually I come back with a few thousand dollars. When we finally did go to the track, me and him, I played two horses and I won $8,443!

SH: You're kidding!

CR: Nope. We were coming back and I'm in the back seat, waving the money around like I'm rich! I gave my mother a thousand, my father a thousand, by the time I got home, I only had about four hundred left! I took them all out to dinner, we were really drinking!

SH: Do you consider yourself a lucky person?

CR: No, I don't think I'm lucky. No, that'll never happen again in a million years! Now when we go down the shore, I'm always borrowing money from my husband!

SH: Tell me one more of your favorite stories about the neighborhood.

CR: Oh, there used to be a Christmas train. Did anyone else tell you about the Christmas train? That used to be awesome! I used to get everybody together, my mother, my sister, my son. When I first met Andy, he said, "Why don't we take little Romeo on the train?" And I said, "To where?" And he said, "To Wilmington and back." It was about an hour ride. They had reindeers

"That's where we used to make out—in the cabooses! If my father'd ever caught me, he'd of killed me! I was about 16. That was our little make-out spot—nobody ever caught us, except once when my father would be riding by when I was just getting out of there."

and everything. They'd give all the kids big stockings with different things for the boys and girls. They gave all the women a box of Whitman chocolates! They gave us all donuts, hot chocolate. The train left from Schuylkill Avenue here,

Christine Rivello at work at the Midtown III Restaurant, Center City

went down to Delaware, then came back. The train went right from the neighborhood. It left from the trestle right at the end of the street here. That's where we used to make out—in the cabooses! If my father'd ever caught me, he'd of killed me! Sometimes we used to just sit in

there, talking. I was about 16. That was our little make-out spot—nobody ever caught us, except once when my father would be riding by when I was just getting out of there. That was funny! They still have that train now, every Christmas. Two years ago we went on that Christmas train.

SH: It sounds like this was a great place to grow up.

CR: We never had any arguments down here. I mean, we used to fight, sure, we used to fight among each other—me and my sister and my cousins. It wasn't a black and white thing, though—we never had no racial trouble down here. We weren't brought up that way, not like down on 29th Street. This was definitely a different neighborhood. No one's even heard of it! When I tell people where I live, they always say, "Where? Where?" If you call a cab down here, you have to tell them like 50 times where to go. People think this is a little deserted neighborhood and when they come down here they say, "I never knew this was here!" It's still a nice neighborhood here, but it's not like it used to be. Whenever I walk down the street and I turn the corner, I think about my brothers and their friends, "do-wopping" on the corner. They used to stand there and they were really good! No one used to mess with me because I had my three brothers. They always looked out for their sisters, even the younger one. The families are really close around here. And you'd better respect an elderly person here! You'd never go home and tell your mother and father, "This one yelled at me," or "That one yelled at me." Because then they'd beat you up again! When I was going to school, you'd never come home and say, "The nuns beat me up," because then your mother and father would beat you up again—really. But my parents are really good—they straightened me out. We don't have a lot of problems around here. I grew up with Jimmy Hudson, with the Gaines family. All good people. Everyone looked out for each other. Once in awhile we had problems when outsiders came in, from the projects or whatever. But mostly it's been a great neighborhood. §

Romeo Rivello

Romeo Rivello on the front porch of his house, 2002

Romeo Rivello was born in the Forgotten Bottom 80 years ago and grew up on Grove St., one of 14 brothers and sisters. His father operated a barbershop for many years on Wharton St. Mr. Rivello attended Audenreid Junior High School, then served in the army during World War II, which claimed the lives of two of his brothers. His wife "married into the Bottom" over 50 years ago, and they raised their five children on Grove St. as well. Mr. Rivello has worked in a number of industries around the neighborhood, but most of his working life was spent at the GE plant at 69th and Elmwood St. He and his wife are stalwart members of the Forgotten Bottom Neighborhood Association.

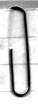
SUSAN HYATT: So how long have you lived in this neighborhood?

ROMEO RIVELLO: For my whole life—80 years. My wife married into the neighborhood, so she's been here about 52 years.

SH: What's special about the neighborhood?

RR: There are lots of friendly people here. My father used to own a barbershop on Wharton Street—he died in 1951. He'd wanted me to take over the barbershop but I just couldn't stand hair—I still can't! We used to have open houses on the holidays. We'd serve food and people would stop by to play cards.

SH: What do you miss from the old days?

RR: The Italian club—Club Mario Bianco. Mario Bianco was a First Captain in World War I. The club was located on Wharton St. between 35th and 36th. We used to run trips to Atlantic City—right from Grays Ferry Avenue! It cost 25 cents round trip in the summer. We'd give out ice cream and soda to everyone. The neighborhood had a lot of Italian, Polish and Irish people then. We all went to King of Peace Church and St. Gabriel's. I was married at King of Peace Church in 1950. When I graduated

> "I worked at the meat-packing house down here—Vogt's—it was called. It was a slaughterhouse, too. They used to slaughter 400 pigs and cows a day. Once I caught ungulate fever from a pig and was in a coma for four days."

from Audenreid Junior High School, I joined the Civilian Conservation Corps. It was during the Depression and the WPA [Works Progress Administration] put everyone to work. I was 16. I was sent to Arizona to work on building a museum near the Grand

Canyon. That was before the Hoover Dam was even built! I did masonry work.

SH: What kinds of jobs did you have after that?

RR: I worked at the meatpacking house down here—Vogt's it was called. It was a slaughterhouse, too. They used to slaughter 400 pigs and cows a day. Once I caught ungulate fever from a pig and was in a coma for four days. After that, I wasn't allowed to work with the animals any more. Then I worked for Reliance Homes, building pre-fabs in Essington until that company went bankrupt. The place where I worked the longest was the GE [General Electric] plant down at 69th and Elmwood Ave. I went to work there right after I got married and I stayed there for 32 years.

SH: What street did you live on when you were growing up?

RR: I grew up over my dad's barbershop on Wharton St. I was one of 14 kids! I was the fifth down in the ages. My sister Juliet is the only one who still lives in the neighborhood. I've always loved this neighborhood and I never wanted to leave. Whenever I go to visit my daughter in Jersey, I can't wait to get home.

> **"I grew up over my dad's barbershop on Wharton St. I was one of 14 kids!"**

My wife didn't grow up the neighborhood. She came from 27th and Reed. She was Irish so my mother taught her how to cook Italian food! We used to have 5 or 6 family-owned grocery stores, right in the neighborhood. Now there's just the big Pathmark on Grays Ferry Avenue. We also had three clubs—St. John's was originally Polish, then Irish. The old Italian club is a Black club now. Even up to the 1980s, we still had some neighborhood stores.

[Romeo's wife, Martha Rivello, joins

Children marching in the streets waving flags at the beginning of WWII

the conversation]: I remember when I first moved here, come 5:00, everyone lined up on the streets to buy pizza, 25 cents a slice!

RR: We raised five kids in this house. We can't believe it now! Now that there's just two of us, we feel as though we don't have enough space. We have seven grandchildren and three great-grandchildren. Our daughter Christine lives around the corner and my sister Juliet is down the street. Our kids went to the neighborhood Catholic schools. In those days, in order to go to King of Peace school, your mother or

RR: Well, we only started it about two years ago. It started up because there was a rumor that they were going to tear down all of our houses. Everyone turned out to find out what was happening. There were over 100 people at that first meeting! After that scare was over, fewer people came to our meetings. This part of the neighborhood was

---

"I lost two brothers, both killed in [World War II]. I was over there, too, and they came to get me and sent me home because I was the only surviving son."

---

your father had to be Italian.

SH: How has the neighborhood changed over the years?

RR: Well, there's more crime in Southwest Philly so people are moving over here. We've never had any problem with crime here. Asian families are moving in from Southwest—we have about five or six families living on this street. They are good neighbors.

SH: How did you get involved with the Forgotten Bottom Neighborhood Association?

always known as "the Bottom." We never saw any troubles down at this end. Even though we were part of Grays Ferry, we didn't have anything here like they had across 34th St.

SH: Mrs. Rivello, what did you think when you first came to this neighborhood?

MR: Well, I always felt at home here. I grew up Irish. We celebrated our 50th wedding anniversary two years ago. We married at King of Peace Church and had our recep-

"... Sure, we had some 'wise guys' down here. They used to patrol the streets! Johnny Stanfa, he was the head of the mob and he was friends with Tony Merlino. They used to meet at that restaurant on the bridge, La Rosa."

tion at St. Theresa. We had a 12-piece string band play for us!

SH: What do you remember about World War II in the neighborhood?

RR: When the war ended, all the kids walked down the street carrying flags. I'd served in England and France. I lost two brothers, both killed in the War. I was over there, too, and they came to get me and sent me home because I was the only surviving son. One of my brothers actually did come home, but he died soon after from injuries. One of my brothers was killed in the invasion of Anzio, the other died of a cerebral hemorrhage after he'd been sent home. It was kill or be killed but I never had to kill anyone.

Romeo Rivello, third from left, on a fishing trip with the Knights of the Red Branch, 1946

The Knights of the Red Branch football team, 1950s

SH: What do you think about the future of the neighborhood?

RR: I think the neighborhood is getting better and better. Since we started the Forgotten Bottom Neighborhood Association, we've had FedEx move in. They cleaned up a crummy factory and junkyard that had been there for years. About five or six years ago, the Pathmark opened. Now they have all these plans to redevelop the Schuylkill River Park and that's going to come down into this area and that will be

another improvement.

SH: I know this is kind of a dubious question to ask, but was the mob ever involved down here?

RR: [laughs] Why are you blushing?

SH: Because it seems like this question is based on a stereotype of Italians!

RR: Maybe, but sure, we had some "wise guys" down here. They used to patrol the streets! Johnny Stanfa, he was the head of the mob and he was friends with Tony Merlino. They used to meet at that restau-

Romeo Rivello in front of his father's barbershop, 1950

always bandaging us up. His real name is Dominic Nappi but everyone in the Bottom calls him "Dr. Dukie."

We've had our share of good and bad times down here in the Bottom but all in all, it's always been a good neighborhood and I think it will always be a good neighborhood.§

"Dr. Dukie" (a.k.a Dominic Nappi) and his wife

rant on the bridge, La Rosa.
SH: Were there any other memorable characters from the Bottom?
RR: Well, there's Dr. Dukie—he grew up on Wharton St. His father was a shoemaker and his mother was a seamstress. We always called him "the Duke" because he was always helping everyone. Even before he became a doctor, he took care of the football team—he was